the
Business Turnaround
& Bankruptcy
KIT

John Ventura

Dearborn™
Trade Publishing
A **Kaplan Professional** Company

Vice President and Publisher: Cynthia A. Zigmund
Senior Managing Editor: Jack Kiburz
Interior Design: Lucy Jenkins
Cover Design: KTK Design Associates
Typesetting: the dotted i

Published by Dearborn Trade Publishing
A Kaplan Professional Company

Library of Congress Cataloging-in-Publication Data

Ventura, John.
    The business turnaround and bankruptcy kit / John Ventura.
      p.   cm.
    Includes index.
    ISBN 0-7931-6044-8 (pbk. : perm. paper)
    1. Bankruptcy—United States—Popular works.   2. Business
failures—Law and legislation—United States—Popular works.   I. Title.
KF1524.6.V463 2003
346.7307′8—dc21

2002155466

Dedication

To Steve Gomez, my brother-in-law, a true survivor and a great guy

Acknowledgments

A heartfelt thanks to Kevin Muir with Turnaround Central in Austin, Texas, and Wayne Fuquay with Wayne Fuquay & Associates in Houston, Texas, for their willingness to share their information and insights regarding the turnaround process. Thanks as well to Tony Gerbino with Bridge Associates, LLC, in Houston.

Also, I want to extend a big thank-you to all my coworkers at my law firm for their understanding and support while I was working on this book.

Contents

Introduction

As a bankruptcy attorney, I meet with the owners of financially struggling businesses every day. Therefore, I know how stressful it is when your business cannot pay all of its bills, its credit is drying up, your best employees are jumping ship for more secure jobs, and you don't know which way to turn. When your business is in crisis, it can be difficult to think straight so you can figure out what to do. That's why I wrote *The Business Turnaround and Bankruptcy Kit*—to explain your options for dealing with your business's troubles and to provide easy-to-understand explanations of each option. Although most of the information in this book assumes that your business is a small, closely held corporation—a corporation that is not publicly traded—I also provide a limited amount of information and advice specific to sole proprietorships. However, if you want more information about filing bankruptcy as a sole proprietorship, see my book, *The Bankruptcy Kit*, 2nd edition (Dearborn Trade Publishing, 1996).

Chapter 1 of *The Business Turnaround and Bankruptcy Kit* introduces the options you have for dealing with a financially troubled business. For example, to save your business, your options include filing a Chapter 11 reorganization bankruptcy or attempting a turnaround, which is a nonjudicial process for reorganizing debt.

The first chapter also covers your options when you don't want to keep your business going or when saving it is not realistic. Those options include selling your business, selling off its assets, and filing a Chapter 7 liquidation bankruptcy.

Subsequent chapters in *The Business Turnaround and Bankruptcy Kit* provide detailed information about the turnaround and bankruptcy options. By reading these chapters, you will learn, among other things, when each option is most appropriate, the kinds of planning your business should do before it pursues a particular option, and what to expect if you decide to pursue a turnaround or a Chapter 11 or Chapter 7 bankruptcy.

I'll guide you through the turnaround and Chapter 11 bankruptcy processes and highlight potential obstacles and problems your business may encounter along the way. In addition, I'll explain why handling your business's turnaround or bankruptcy is never a good idea and tell you how to find a qualified turnaround or bankruptcy firm to help your business.

I'll also address the emotional aspects of dealing with a business in financial crisis in this book. In my experience, when the owners of financially troubled businesses experience a lot of stress and anxiety, they have difficulty making wise and timely decisions for their business. Therefore, to help you cope with the emotions you may be feeling right now, I'll review the ways that your business's problems may be affecting you, highlight the most common signs of emotional overload, and provide practical suggestions for how to alleviate stress and worry. I'll also discuss ways to overcome the feelings of panic and self-doubt that business owners in your situation often experience.

I'll provide advice for keeping your cool when you have to deal with demanding creditors and, because sooner or later your employees will be aware of your business's troubles, I'll provide suggestions for how to keep them motivated during its financial crisis. In addition, I'll highlight issues to think about regarding when to tell your employees about the troubles.

The Business Turnaround and Bankruptcy Kit also provides a glossary of words and terms you may encounter when your business is in bankruptcy and samples of the various legal forms a bankruptcy attorney will have to complete and file with the court, depending on whether your business files a Chapter 11 or Chapter 7 bankruptcy.

1

Assessing Your Options When Your Business Is in Financial Trouble

When your business is in trouble, the sooner you recognize that fact, the more options you will have for dealing with problems and saving your business—if that is your goal. On the other hand, if you wait too long to face facts and take decisive action, you may be left with no other option than to shut down your business. Furthermore, the longer you wait, the more likely it is that your personal finances will be affected, assuming that you are personally liable for any of your business's debts. To protect your personal assets from your business's creditors, you may have to file for personal bankruptcy.

This chapter reviews the most common signs of business trouble, so that you will know when to take action. It also provides an overview of the various options you have for resolving your business's financial troubles, although some of them may not be appropriate for your particular business. Those options include:

- Selling your business
- Selling off your business assets
- Liquidating your business through bankruptcy
- Saving your business through either a turnaround or a reorganization bankruptcy

The chapter also highlights key factors to consider when you are deciding which option is the best one for your business. Subsequent chapters discuss turnarounds, as well as reorganization and liquidation bankruptcies in detail.

Your Business Is in Trouble If ...

Every business is different, so the signs of financial trouble for one business may not apply to another. However, certain problems most often tend to be warning signs, regardless of the type of business, its size, industry, etc. For example, your business is probably in trouble if:

- It has experienced a decline in sales over the past several quarters and/or sales that are not at the level you budgeted for. The decline may have occurred because your business does not have enough cash to fund its sales, demand for its products or services has fallen off, your business has been affected by an economic slowdown in its particular industry or in the economy at large, or there are deficiencies in its sales and marketing program, among others reasons.
- It has lost one or more important customers and has not been able to replace the income that these customers provided.
- It is having trouble paying its rent or mortgage.
- It is struggling to make payroll.
- It has been hit with substantial, unexpected expenses that it does not have the funds to pay.
- It has begun to fall behind on its debts and cannot get caught up.
- Some of its accounts have been turned over to collection agencies.
- Some of its secured creditors have asked for more collateral.
- Creditors and suppliers have tightened their credit policies with your business or will no longer extend credit to your business.
- You are worried that the bank may cancel your business's line of credit or refuse to renew its current loan.
- The bank is threatening to call your business loan.
- Creditors are threatening your business with legal action.
- It has begun to fall behind on its tax obligations. For example, your business may be using the payroll tax money it collects to fund its operations rather than sending the money to the IRS.
- Some of its key managers have quit.

If you ignore the signs of trouble on the previous list, your business's financial troubles will almost certainly go from bad to worse. For example:

> ## WARNING
>
> It is human nature to want to ignore difficult problems and put off dealing with them. Therefore, you may be tempted to minimize your business's problems or assume that if you wait long enough, the problems will become less serious or maybe even go away. They won't.

- The IRS may seize its assets, levy its bank accounts, and pursue other avenues of enforced collection action.
- Creditors and suppliers may sue your business to get the money they are owed.
- Its secured creditors may take back their collateral. Losing assets that are essential to the operation of your business could be a fatal blow to it.
- It may be evicted from its office space.
- Your employees may sue your business for unpaid wages.
- Your business may not have enough cash to purchase the supplies, raw materials, services, etc., it needs to continue operating.

Assessing Your Options

When your business's finances are headed downhill, your first decision should be whether or not you want to remain in business. This is an important decision, so spend time thinking about it, and when you do, try to put aside your emotions and your ego. Also, don't let your pride get in the way of making the decision that is best for you, as well as for your family, because they will be affected by it. Among other things, you should consider:

- How hard will it be for you to raise the money you need to keep your business going?
- Do you have what it takes to save your business? Running a small business is hard enough, but trying to save a business that is in trouble and run it at the same time can be a monumental challenge, which is what you will have to do if you opt for a turnaround or a Chapter 11 bankruptcy. Don't underestimate the

amount of your time—not to mention the amount of money—it will take for you to meet that challenge. And remember, there is no guarantee that your efforts will succeed.

- Do you really want to save your business? Don't even think about trying unless you are 100 percent committed to the job. A half-hearted effort will almost certainly mean failure.
- Is trying to save your business fair to your family? Given the effort involved, you may have little or no energy to devote to your family at the end of each day and on weekends, and the emotions and pressure you experience may take a toll on your family relationships. Therefore, it is a good idea to involve your spouse or partner in the decision-making process and to be sensitive to his or her concerns.

If you decide that you want to save your business and that the potential benefits outweigh the sacrifices you and your family will have to make, you have two options for achieving that goal: a turnaround or a Chapter 11 reorganization bankruptcy. Chapter 3 explains how turnarounds work, and Chapter 4 introduces you to the bankruptcy process in general. Chapter 5 provides specific information about the Chapter 11 bankruptcy process.

WARNING

Pursuing a turnaround or a reorganization bankruptcy will cost your business considerable money. Therefore, the sooner you begin figuring out how your business will pay for it, the better your chances of success.

If you decide that you do not want to stay in business, regardless of the reasons, you have four options for ending it. You can:

1. Sell your business as a going concern.
2. Sell off the individual assets in your business.
3. Just shut down your business.
4. End your business by liquidating its assets through a Chapter 7 bankruptcy.

Professional Advice and Assistance Required

When you have poured your heart and soul into a business, being objective about its prospects for the future and how best to deal with its problems can be difficult. For example, you may be so emotionally attached to your business that you cannot put enough distance between it and you to be realistic about whether the business is worth saving—or if it even *can* be saved. Furthermore, even if you are able to make this assessment, you may not have the knowledge or the skills required to develop and implement a practical plan of action for implementing your decision. Therefore, as soon as your business begins to experience any of the problems listed earlier in this chapter in the "Your Business Is in Trouble If . . ." section, you should schedule a meeting with your business's CPA (certified public accountant), a small business bankruptcy attorney, or a turnaround firm. These resources can help you analyze the fundamental health of your business and determine whether it can be saved and what saving it will probably take.

Here is a summary of the kinds of assistance each professional can offer you and your business:

- A CPA can take a hard look at the state of your business's finances and may be able to recommend ways to improve them. However, most CPAs do not have the skills to evaluate your management abilities or the abilities of your top managers or to assess the appropriateness of your business's organizational structure, the effectiveness of your operations, the viability of your business's services or products, whether any personnel changes are necessary, and so on.

WARNING

If your business's CPA has not already alerted you to the deteriorating state of your business's finances, look for a new CPA.

- A turnaround firm can help you pinpoint the origins of your business's financial difficulties, assess what it will take to save your business, negotiate with your business's creditors and suppliers, and devise a plan to address the business's problems and free up cash, so that your business can become profitable. If a turnaround is not a viable option for your business, the firm will probably advise your business to file either a reorganization or a liquidation bankruptcy. Many turnaround firms have a bankruptcy attorney on staff or have a relationship with a bankruptcy attorney, so they can either handle your business's bankruptcy or refer you to an attorney who can.

• A bankruptcy attorney can help you determine if there is anything your business can do to avoid bankruptcy—attempt a turnaround for example. Some bankruptcy firms also do turnarounds. If the attorney decides that bankruptcy is your business's best option, he or she will advise you about which type of bankruptcy your business should file, whether a Chapter 11 reorganization or a Chapter 7 liquidation.

WARNING

Your business's financial woes may have developed because you are not a good business manager and do not have adequate management skills, or because your business has outgrown your ability to run it. Therefore, if you truly want to save your business, difficult as it may be for you emotionally, stay open to the possibility that you may have to change the role that you play in your business—give up certain responsibilities or even turn over the day-to-day management to someone else, for example.

Reviewing Your Options

This section of Chapter 1 highlights the various options that are available to financially troubled businesses. As outlined earlier, if you decide to end your business, you have four basic options:

1. Sell it as a going concern.
2. Sell off its assets.
3. Shut it down.
4. Liquidate its assets through a Chapter 7 bankruptcy.

Sell Your Business

Selling your business is a good option when your business's finances have not deteriorated to the point that filing a Chapter 7 liquidation bankruptcy is an immediate necessity. It would be a necessity, for example, if your business's secured creditors were preparing to take back their collateral, or if your business owed back taxes and the IRS were about to seize its assets.

Your business may be a candidate for sale if all or some of the following apply:

- It has enough cash to continue operating until you find a qualified buyer for it.
- Despite its current problems, your business has the potential for future profits.
- The assets your business owns are likely to increase in value in coming years.
- Its tangible assets would be of value to another owner.
- Its intangible assets would be of value to another owner. Examples of intangible assets include a well-established business name, a loyal customer base, a solid reputation, a good business location, or well-trained, satisfied employees, among other things.

HOT TIP

Potential buyers for your business may include its competitors, customers, and entrepreneurs looking for a good investment opportunity, among others.

HOT TIP

Sometimes, before a financially faltering business can be sold, it must go through a turnaround, or Chapter 11 reorganization, so that it will be attractive to potential buyers and can be sold for a good price.

Ordinarily, you will get the best price for your business and sell it faster if you work with a broker rather than try to handle the sale yourself. Business brokers know how to:

- Set a realistic asking price for a business.
- Locate qualified potential buyers.
- Negotiate the terms of sale.
- Handle all of the sales paperwork.

Hire a broker who has specific experience selling businesses similar to yours in terms of business type, industry, annual revenues, number of employees, etc. The broker will take his or her fee from the sale proceeds. Typically, the fee will be a percentage of the selling price.

To find a reputable broker in your area, go to the Web site of the International Business Brokers Association at <www.ibba.org/> or ask for referrals from your business associates, the trade or professional associations you belong to, your local chamber of commerce, your CPA, and your banker. Also, there may be an association of business brokers in your state that can refer you to brokers in your area. Check in your local Yellow Pages and search the Internet to find such an association.

Once you find a business broker to hire, get a signed contract from the broker that spells out the specific services he or she will provide your business, the duration of services, the percentage commission the broker will earn for selling your business, and all other terms of the relationship.

HOT TIP

Avoid a long-term contract with a business broker. A six- to nine-month contract with an option to renew is usually best. The risk of agreeing to a longer contract is that if the broker is ineffective or you have difficulty working together, you may not be able to get out of the contract before its term is up without hiring an attorney.

> ## HOT TIP
>
> When you negotiate the terms of your business's broker contract, consider reserving the right to sell the business yourself and paying the broker a smaller commission, or no commission at all, if you do.

Sell Your Business's Assets

If there is not a ready market for your business as a going concern, you may be able to pay its debts, especially any debts that you are personally liable for, by selling your business's assets individually. This option makes sense if:

- Your business has tangible assets with significant market value —equipment, machinery, vehicles, furniture, etc.—and you believe that you can sell those assets relatively quickly. If it takes too long to find buyers, and if your business's finances continue to deteriorate, filing for bankruptcy may become a necessity for your business.
- Your business does not have a lot of secured debt, and the assets that collateralize the debt are worth more than the outstanding balances on the debt.
- Your business has a low debt-to-asset ratio—the lower the better.
- Your business's secured creditors are not threatening to take back their collateral.
- You are personally liable for all or a significant number of your business's debts.

If you are confident that you can sell your business assets quickly without professional help, it's a good idea to hire an appraiser to value them, or to value the assets you believe are worth the most. The assets will sell faster if they are priced right.

Potential buyers for your business's assets include its competitors and companies that offer a product or service that is complementary to or similar to your business's.

You can reach these potential buyers by:

- Using word-of-mouth advertising.
- Placing an ad in the publications of the trade and professional organizations you belong to.
- Advertising in your local daily newspaper or business journal.
- Using the eBay Web site. If you go to the home page for business products and services at this site (www.ebay.com/catindex /business), you will see that it features a wide range of items for sale, including office products and equipment, electronics, construction and industrial equipment, and retail supplies, among other items. You can even sell your business on eBay.

WARNING

Don't wait until your business is in dire circumstances to find buyers for its assets, because a quick sale may become more important than holding out for the best deal.

If you decide you would prefer to hire a professional to market your business's assets, your bank can probably provide you with the names of reputable business liquidators. If you are selling specialized equipment, furniture, or other items that are unique to your business's industry or to your type of business, work with a liquidator who specializes in selling such assets rather than with a general business liquidator.

Shut It Down

Another option when you want to end your business is to just shut it down rather than filing a Chapter 7 liquidation bankruptcy. If you pursue this option, your business should return the assets that it used as collateral to its secured creditors, especially if those assets are worth a significant amount of money or if the creditors with liens on those assets are willing to forgive any deficiency your business may owe to them.

If your business owns any unsecured assets that have a market value, sell those assets and use the proceeds either to pay any deficiencies your business may owe to its secured creditors or to pay off other

---

WARNING

If you want to sell an asset that collateralizes a business debt and you believe that the asset will not sell for enough to pay off the loan balance, your business must get the lender's permission to sell it. The lender may be willing to forgive the *deficiency*—the difference between the loan balance and what the asset sells for. Otherwise, the buyer of the asset cannot get clear title to the asset until the deficiency has been paid off in full.

HOT TIP

If a creditor agrees to take assets in lieu of cash or if it agrees to forgive a deficiency, get the agreement in writing.

---

debts. Another option for dealing with the money your business owes is to let creditors take your business's unsecured assets in lieu of cash.

Closing down your business avoids the cost and stigma of filing for bankruptcy. However, this option comes with some potential risks. For example:

- Creditors who are not paid all the money they are entitled to may sue your business.
- Your business's creditors may come after your personal assets to collect the money they are entitled to if you are personally liable for its unpaid debts.
- If you hope to begin a new business in the near future, especially one that is similar to the one you shut down or in the same industry, creditors and suppliers may not want to work with your new business, because they may be angry about the way they were treated by your former business.

File a Liquidation Bankruptcy

When you liquidate your business through a Chapter 7 bankruptcy, a court-appointed trustee will take control of its assets, sell them, and distribute the sale proceeds to your business's creditors in order to pay as many of its debts as possible.

Filing for a Chapter 7 bankruptcy is a good idea when:

- Your business has little or no cash flow.
- Your business's creditors are not willing to work with your business so that it can restructure its debts.
- Your business has little chance of becoming profitable.
- Your business owes a lot of money to unsecured creditors and cannot afford to pay those debts.
- Your business owes a substantial amount of money to the IRS.
- Your business owns few if any assets of value.

Chapter 4 in this book provides an overview of the bankruptcy liquidation process. Chapter 6 takes you step-by-step through the process.

Options for Saving Your Business

You have two basic options if you want to keep your business going: pursue a turnaround or put your business into a Chapter 11 reorganization bankruptcy. Although both options have the same goal, they differ in some important ways that are highlighted in this chapter. For additional information on turnarounds, read Chapter 3. For more detailed information on Chapter 11 bankruptcy, read Chapters 4 and 5.

W A R N I N G

When an important secured creditor—your business's bank, for example—is aware of the seriousness of your business's financial problems, it may give you an ultimatum: Hire a turnaround firm, or the bank will take back its collateral.

Overview of the Chapter 11 Bankruptcy Process

Chapter 11 bankruptcy is an appropriate alternative for businesses that are fundamentally sound and that have the potential to become profitable. The Chapter 11 process gives you an opportunity to reorganize your business's debts and resolve the problems that have contributed to those problems while your business is under the protection of the federal bankruptcy court. Once your business's bankruptcy begins, the court will issue an *automatic stay,* which is a type of injunction. It prohibits most of your business's creditors from trying to collect their money while your business is in bankruptcy.

Federal law defines and governs the bankruptcy process. Among other things, the law requires that your business:

- Treat certain kinds of debts in specific ways.
- Meet specific deadlines.
- Follow specific procedures during bankruptcy, including filing certain paperwork with the court and preparing monthly reports for the court.

These requirements limit your business's freedom to deal with its debts, and they add to the stress and expense of the Chapter 11 process.

Furthermore, because the law gives so much power to Chapter 11 creditors, once the bankruptcy begins, your business's creditors can create so many delays and expenses for your business that it may be forced to convert the bankruptcy to a Chapter 7 liquidation. In fact, this happens in many business Chapter 11 reorganizations.

WARNING

If your business does not comply with the requirements of federal bankruptcy law, the court may dismiss its Chapter 11 bankruptcy, and your business may have to liquidate through a Chapter 7 liquidation.

> ### WARNING
>
> Although bankruptcy is more commonplace than it used to be, it still has a stigma associated with it. For example, some creditors and suppliers may be less willing to work with your business after it has filed for Chapter 11, and if any of your business's customers get wind of its bankruptcy, they may not want to do business with you anymore. Your business will have to work extra hard to overcome the stigma that comes with bankruptcy.

How a Turnaround Works

A turnaround gives your business a chance to pay off its debts, negotiate with its creditors, address the problems that caused its financial troubles, and become profitable without the involvement of the bankruptcy court. Compared to a Chapter 11 bankruptcy, a turnaround gives your business more freedom to deal with its debts and no legal deadlines to adhere to; however, in a turnaround your business will not be protected by the automatic stay.

Your business may be a candidate for a turnaround if:

- It can generate enough cash to continue operating during the turnaround process and pay for the turnaround, too.
- There is an adequate market for its products or services.
- Its creditors are willing to hold off on taking legal action to collect the money your business owes to them, including not taking back their collateral.
- Its creditors are willing to give your business the concessions it needs to accomplish a turnaround.

Most businesses hire a turnaround firm to plan and manage their turnarounds. However, if your business cannot afford to pay a firm to manage its turnaround from start to finish, it may be able to find a firm that will diagnose the causes of its problems, prepare its turnaround plan, and then coach you through the implementation of that plan.

> ## WARNING
>
> If the market for your business's products or services is depressed, and its competitors have responded to the situation by slashing their prices, paring back their operations, consolidating, etc., it is probably too late for a turnaround.

The typical turnaround involves the following five basic steps, some of which will be carried out concurrently:

1. Diagnose the root causes of your business's problems.
2. Identify ready sources of cash, so that your business can fund its operations during the turnaround and also pay for the turnaround.
3. Prepare a turnaround plan. The plan will detail how your business will be saved.
4. Renegotiate the terms of your business's debts and take on new debt as necessary.
5. Take other steps to improve your business's finances and operations in order to stabilize the business and make it profitable.

> ## HOT TIP
>
> Some business owners use a turnaround to prepare their businesses for sale, so that at a minimum they can pay off the debt for which they are personally liable.

When you are evaluating whether or not a turnaround is your business's best option, it is important that you understand the potential disadvantages of the process so that you can balance them against its benefits. Those disadvantages include:

- There is no automatic stay, so your business's creditors are free to try to collect on their debts while the turnaround is being planned and implemented. However, if creditors believe that your business has a good chance for a successful turnaround, they are more apt to hold off on their collection actions.
- Creditors are not bound by the terms of your business's turnaround plan, unless they have signed agreements with your business to that effect.
- If your business has a lot of creditors spread out over a wide geographic area, negotiating the terms of a turnaround can be time consuming and cumbersome.

2

Dealing with Stress and Emotion When Your Business Is in Crisis

It can be lonely, stressful, and sometimes downright scary to own a business that is in a state of financial crisis. Among other things, you may feel overwhelmed by anxiety and have a hard time sleeping, and you may struggle to keep panic and self-doubt at bay.

Feeling anxious, stressed out, and overwhelmed are natural responses to your situation, considering all that you have invested in your business—your hopes and dreams and countless hours of your time, not to mention money. In fact, you may be personally liable for some of your business's debts. Maybe you helped finance the business with a home equity loan or with your credit cards, or perhaps you provided a lender a personal guarantee. Furthermore, your family may be having trouble paying its bills, because it relies on income from your business.

No wonder you are stressed out! However, too much stress and anxiety will make it difficult, if not impossible, for you to think clearly and rationally about how to deal with your business's problems and will hamper your decision making. Worst case scenario, the decisions you make will exacerbate your business's problems, not make them better, and you may end up missing your window of opportunity for saving your business. Therefore, this chapter provides suggestions for reducing the stress in your life, so that you can tackle your business's problems with a clear mind. It also offers suggestions for countering the panic and self-doubt that a failing business can trigger. In addition, the chapter provides advice for staying calm, cool, and collected when you are dealing with angry, demanding creditors, and discusses the potential impact of your business's problems on your employees.

Recognizing the Signs of Too Much Stress

A little stress in life can be a good thing. It can help keep you motivated, energized, and focused on the task at hand. However, too much stress can take a toll on you physically as well as emotionally. Among other things, stress may make it difficult for you to sleep and cause you to be more susceptible to colds, everyday bugs, and viruses, or more serious illnesses, like high blood pressure, heart attacks, strokes, and even cancer. Too much stress can also cause you to eat too much or too little, to abuse alcohol or drugs, and to become seriously depressed.

Feeling stressed out can also take its toll on your personal and family lives. It may cause you to snap at your kids, fight with your spouse or partner, withdraw from your friends and family, be irritable and impatient at work, and stop doing the things that you enjoy. All of these responses are apt to create even more stress in your life and make you even more susceptible to stress-related problems: a vicious and life-destroying cycle. Therefore, to help you stay calm, think logically about your business, and keep the rest of your life in balance as much as possible, here are some suggestions for how to reduce stress:

- Whenever you begin to feel overwhelmed and panicky, stop what you are doing, close your eyes, and breathe slowly and deeply for a couple minutes. You can do this anywhere—at your desk, at home, in the shower.
- Meditate. Even five to ten minutes of mediation can make you feel calmer. If you don't know how to meditate, learn by purchasing a guided meditation tape or CD, by taking a class on meditation, or by reading a book on the topic.
- Exercise. Ride your bike, jog, use a treadmill, lift weights, play basketball, swim. Even a brisk walk can help calm your nerves and clear your head. Get moving and sweat your stress away!
- Practice yoga. Because the popularity of yoga has increased in recent years, you can probably find a yoga class close to where you live or work—at the health club you belong to, the YWCA or YMCA in your area, your local community college, or at a

nearby yoga center, for example. There are many different types of yoga, so explore what is available in order to find the yoga class that is right for you. If you can't find a convenient yoga class, do yoga at home using a yoga videotape or DVD. You may also be able to find a yoga class on a local cable channel.

- Schedule an appointment with a mental health professional, such as a psychologist, licensed counselor, or a social worker. The mental health professional can help you get a handle on your feelings and suggest healthy ways for you to deal with them. Some professionals specialize in stress reduction and management.

H O T   T I P

If your business troubles are taking a toll on your relationship with your spouse or partner, get counseling if you are not able to work things out on your own. Counseling sessions can offer both of you a safe and neutral place to express your fears and worries and to figure out ways to support one another during this difficult time.

- Take time out for fun. Don't give up the things that you enjoy just because your business is in trouble. During tough times, having fun can help you develop and maintain a positive attitude. Therefore, pursue activities that give you pleasure, whether they include watching a movie, reading a book, enjoying a hobby, playing a sport, spending time with your children, playing music, gardening, etc. Pleasurable activities will provide you with a beneficial respite from your business troubles and help you relax.
- Spend time with the people you care about. When you are feeling overwhelmed by problems, it is easy to shut down emotionally and cut yourself off from family and friends. However, isolating yourself from the people you care about and who care about you will almost certainly increase the amount of stress you feel. Plus, the simple act of verbalizing your worries and concerns to someone else can reduce the power those things

have over you and lighten the burden of your business's troubles. Furthermore, the people you share with may be able to help you cope better by giving you a more helpful perspective about yourself and about what is happening to your business. Finally, the knowledge that there are people in your life who care about you, regardless of what condition your business is in, and who don't judge you by its success or failure, can be comforting and help sustain you through tough times.

WARNING

When you are preoccupied by your business's financial problems, it can be easy to focus just on them at your own expense. Don't fall into that trap! Making time for yourself will help you stay healthy and focused and in the end will improve your decision making.

- Write down your feelings. You don't have to be a gifted writer to put your feelings on paper, and no one will grade what you write—your writings are just for you. What you write can be as simple as creating a list of your thoughts in a journal every day. Not only is putting pen to paper a healthy way to deal with your emotions when your business is on a downward slide, but the process of writing may even help you clarify your thoughts and make decisions.

WARNING

If you keep your thoughts and feelings bottled up inside, your business's problems may begin to seem bigger than they really are and more difficult to deal with than they may actually be. So express your thoughts and feelings by writing about them and by talking about them to the people who care about you.

- Pamper yourself. Do something totally self-indulgent once in a while. Take a long hot bath, curl up on the couch with a good book, take a nap, get a massage, get an acupuncture treatment, schedule a pedicure, watch your favorite sports show, etc.

Don't Give In to Self-Doubt

Self-doubt can be another big enemy when you are faced with a financially struggling business. Once your business's troubles begin, you may experience a crisis of confidence, questioning your judgment, your business skills, your past decisions, and your ability to make decisions in the future. You may become immobilized by self-doubt and, as a result, unable to address your business's problems in a timely, effective manner. Worst-case scenario, your lack of confidence will end up costing you your business, even though your business could have been saved if you had not doubted your abilities and had acted decisively.

When feelings of self-doubt begin to surface, here are some ways to banish them:

- Think back to difficult challenges you faced successfully in the past. Draw strength and resolve from your memories and apply them to your current troubles.
- Remind yourself that you are not the first person to own a business with serious financial problems, and that you won't be the last. Countless other business owners who were no more talented or well informed than you are have dealt with the very same problems your business now faces, and they had to make the very same decisions you must make. In other words, if they could do it, so can you!
- Don't keep your feelings of self-doubt to yourself out of embarrassment. They will only fester and grow. Get the support and reassurance you need by sharing your feelings with your spouse or partner, a close friend, or with a trusted business associate. These people can help you put your problems in perspective and bolster your self-confidence. They may even be able to help facilitate your decision making.
- Create a doable list of the steps necessary to resolve your business's problems. Whenever possible, set realistic deadlines for each of the actions on your list. Breaking down an overwhelming challenge into a series of small steps can make the challenge

seem less daunting and can help you feel more able to meet the challenge.

- Get mental health counseling if you experience a crisis of confidence so serious that you cannot make decisions.

Keep Your Cool with Your Business's Creditors

When you are feeling edgy and anxious about your business, it can be a real challenge to stay cool when frustrated, angry creditors begin to call demanding their money and maybe even threatening legal action. Whether you decide your business will pursue a turnaround or file for bankruptcy, the firm you hire to help will deal with the creditors for you. Until then, the responsibility for dealing with angry, upset creditors may fall squarely on your shoulders, even if you have employees who handle your business's accounts payable. Therefore, it is important that you do not alienate your creditors any more than they already are. The success of your business's turnaround or reorganization bankruptcy will depend in part on your creditors' good will and cooperation.

WARNING

Lying to a creditor can be dangerous. You may destroy your credibility with the creditor and so anger the creditor that it will take back its collateral, foreclose on your business, sue your business, etc.

Try not to act defensive when you have to deal with an unhappy creditor, and don't argue with the creditor even if the creditor becomes angry or confrontational. Instead, politely let the creditor know that you appreciate its situation, and that you are actively working to resolve your business's financial problems. If you tell the creditor that your business will send it a check for at least some of what it owes to the creditor, do not promise more money than your business can realistically afford to pay, and never promise to send money just to end an unpleasant conversation.

> ## W A R N I N G
>
> If filing for bankruptcy is a strong possibility for your business, do not pay one creditor at the expense of your business's other creditors during the 90-day period prior to the start of the bankruptcy.

When you are deciding which creditors to pay and how much to pay each, bear in mind the relative importance of one creditor compared to another. For example, if your business owes money on a secured debt, and the collateral for that debt is essential to your business, then the secured creditor associated with that debt belongs on the top of your "bills to be paid" stack. It is a high-priority debt. If you assign that creditor a low priority, it may take back its collateral, and the loss of that asset may cripple your business.

Other creditors that belong at the top of the stack are the companies that are essential to your business's continued operation—key suppliers, for example. Also, be sure to treat any financial obligations that you have personally guaranteed as top priorities, because the creditors associated with those debts can come after your personal assets if your business does not pay them.

Help Your Employees through Stressful Times

Sooner or later, your employees will realize that your business is experiencing financial problems. The news will probably spread quickly, because your employees are likely to talk among themselves. Inevitably, they will begin to speculate about your business's future and about the security of their jobs. As a result, your employees' morale and productivity may suffer, and some employees may leave your business for more secure jobs. This can be bad news for your business if you plan to save it, because experienced employees who can deliver a quality product or service are essential to a successful turnaround or reorganization bankruptcy. Therefore, you should decide as quickly as possible what you are going to do about your business—shut it down, file for bankruptcy, attempt a turnaround, etc.—so that you can minimize the damage its problems are doing to your business's people as well as financial resources.

Meanwhile, you must also decide how much to tell your employees about your business troubles as well as when and how to tell them what your plans are for the business. There is no one right time or way to convey this information. In fact, until you know whether you are going to end your business or try to keep it going, you may have to maintain a delicate balancing act. In large part, your decision regarding how to deal with your employees will depend on your business's culture and on your own management style. For example, if you have an informal management style and your business is built on openness and teamwork, you will probably want to level with your employees sooner than you will if your business is formal and hierarchical. These issues and considerations argue for getting professional help and advice for your business as soon as possible, so that you can figure out sooner rather than later the best way to resolve your business's problems.

WARNING

If there is not already a sense of teamwork and sharing in your business, don't try to create one in the midst of the stress and turmoil that comes with a failing business. It won't work.

HOT TIP

If you hire a turnaround firm, it will meet with your employees early on in the turnaround process to explain the whys and hows of your business's turnaround and to answer their questions. The firm will also provide your employees with periodic updates throughout the turnaround process.

If you want to try to save your business, regardless of whether you opt for a turnaround or bankruptcy, you will face the challenge of how to keep your employees committed and motivated at the same time that you will probably be asking them to do more with less. Although the turnaround firm or bankruptcy attorney will provide you with advice about how to handle this challenge, here are some suggestions:

- Recognize employees who perform "above and beyond the call of duty," even if the recognition is as small as a thank-you.
- Let your employees know that you appreciate *all* of their efforts, and that you realize that each of them is key to saving your business.
- Provide key employees with salary increases if you can afford to, or tie future increases to your business reaching certain milestones along the road to financial recovery.
- Sponsor periodic potluck meals, picnics, or other fun events for your employees.
- Ask your employees to provide you with suggestions for things they can do to cut costs and improve quality and productivity, etc. If you use any of their suggestions, provide them with a special award—a gift certificate or flowers, for example.
- Hold periodic meetings to update your employees on the status of your efforts to save your business and to let them know what you need from them.

Saving Your Business with a Turnaround

Chapter 1 identified the two basic options you have for saving your failing business and explained under what general circumstances each option is feasible. The two options are (1) put your business into a Chapter 11 reorganization bankruptcy or (2) try to reorganize your business informally, without the court's involvement, by attempting a turnaround.

This chapter provides more detailed information about turnarounds. Among other things, the chapter highlights the main differences between a turnaround and a Chapter 11 bankruptcy, reviews the pros and cons of trying to handle a turnaround yourself versus hiring a turnaround firm to help you, and explains how to find a reputable turnaround firm. It also provides an overview of the turnaround process, including information about the kinds of concessions that your business will probably need from its creditors and suppliers and information about the various cost-cutting measures the turnaround firm will want to implement.

Turnarounds and Reorganization Bankruptcies: What's the Difference?

Turnarounds and reorganization bankruptcies share three basic goals:

1. Resolve the problems of a financially troubled business.
2. Pay off the business's debts.
3. Put the business on the road to profitability.

However, the two processes differ in some important ways. The following list summarizes the key differences between the two and highlights the potential advantages of a turnaround compared to bankruptcy:

*   The Chapter 11 bankruptcy process is a formal process for reorganizing your business debts and making your business profitable. It is governed by federal bankruptcy law and involves specific timetables, deadlines, procedures, and reporting, including requirements for how your business must deal with certain types of debts. A turnaround, on the other hand, is an informal reorganization that is not governed by a specific federal or state law. Therefore, your business has more freedom and flexibility to deal with its problems, can establish its own timetables and deadlines, and does not have to spend precious time and money preparing reports for the court and filing paperwork, etc.
*   Creditors usually get more money in a turnaround than in a Chapter 11 bankruptcy.
*   Bankruptcy is a public process, which means that the paperwork your business files with the courts is a matter of public record. Therefore, anyone who wants to can review that information. Also, anyone who wants to can attend your business's bankruptcy hearings. Furthermore, the fact that your business has filed for bankruptcy may be published in your local daily or business journal. A turnaround, on the other hand, is a private process.
*   A turnaround tends to bring less stigma to a business than a bankruptcy does.

Despite the advantages of pursuing a turnaround rather than a bankruptcy, it is apt to cost your business more than a Chapter 11. If your business is very small—a mom-and-pop operation, for example, with no more than 15 employees, 15 or fewer creditors, and no more than $500,000 in debt—a Chapter 11 bankruptcy will probably cost your business between $10,000 and $25,000. A larger small business with more employees, creditors, and debt will probably spend between $30,000 and $50,000 on its Chapter 11. However, many Chapter 11 bankruptcies cost considerably more, especially when a business's creditors are hostile to it, and there is a lot of litigation involved.

On the other hand, the typical small business turnaround usually costs at least $50,000, although it could cost less or more. Factors that will influence its cost include the size of your business, the complexity of its problems, the number of creditors involved, the number of turnaround firm staff who are actively involved in the turnaround, and the specific types of expertise your business needs, among other things. However, if you decide to handle the implementation phase of the turnaround yourself, in consultation with a turnaround firm, you can reduce the total cost of the turnaround. This is particularly true if your business's creditors are willing and ready to help make its turnaround a success.

Your Options for Accomplishing a Turnaround

If you want to save your business through a turnaround, you have three options for achieving that goal:

1. Plan and manage the turnaround yourself.
2. Hire a turnaround firm to plan and execute your business's turnaround, from start to finish.
3. Hire a turnaround firm to identify the reasons for your business's financial problems and to develop a turnaround plan for your business, and then implement the plan yourself using the firm as your "coach."

The rest of this section outlines the pros and cons of each option.

Do It Yourself

Doing your own turnaround is almost never advisable, for many reasons. Here are some of the most important:

- You may not have the financial, management, legal, and negotiation knowledge and skills that are essential to a successful turnaround. In fact, your lack of these things may be at least partially responsible for your business's problems.
- A successful turnaround usually involves concessions from creditors. For example, your business may need its creditors to agree to let it make interest-only payments for a while and to agree to hold off on any collection actions they may be considering. However, if the creditors have lost confidence in your

management abilities, or your business has lost credibility with them because of past unmet promises, the only way creditors may be willing to work with your business is if you hire a reputable turnaround firm.

- If new financing is essential to your business's turnaround, traditional lenders may be reluctant to loan money if you are in charge of the turnaround. You also may be unfamiliar with lenders in the business of making loans to financially distressed companies. Therefore, you will not be able to secure the funds your business needs to have a successful turnaround.

- You may be too close to your business to be able to objectively assess why it is having problems. This is particularly true if you are part of the problem. For example, like many small business owners, you may be great at identifying a marketable idea and turning it into a business, but you may be terrible at managing the business day-to-day or at coping with its growing pains once the business begins to achieve success.

WARNING

If you handle your own business turnaround, you risk making its problems so much worse that your business can't be saved even through a Chapter 11 bankruptcy.

Another risk of trying to handle your own turnaround, even if you have the requisite knowledge and skills, is that your emotions may get in the way of doing what needs to be done. For example, saving your business may mean laying off and demoting employees who are related to you, who have become your friends, or who have worked long and loyally for your business. As a result, you may not be able to carry out the layoffs and demotions, or you may delay taking those steps for so long that your business is further damaged, maybe to the point that bankruptcy becomes a necessity and not an option.

Use a Turnaround Firm to Handle the Entire Turnaround

As you probably realize after reading the previous section of this chapter, there are some important advantages to hiring a turnaround firm to plan and manage your business's turnaround. One of the most important is that a turnaround firm has the knowledge, expertise, and experience to save your business. Therefore, once your business has hired the firm, it can "hit the ground running" and move quickly and decisively to try to do that. This is significant, because in a turnaround situation, delays and missteps can be costly and even fatal to a financially troubled business.

Another important advantage to working with a turnaround firm is that its employees can be dispassionate about your business because they have no emotional ties to it. Therefore, they will be better able than you to accurately diagnose the root causes of your business's problems and develop a realistic plan for resolving those problems and dealing with your business's debts.

Credibility with your business's creditors is another important benefit to working with a turnaround firm. Creditors are apt to view the fact that your business has hired a turnaround firm as evidence that your business is committed to dealing with its problems. As a result, they may be more willing to help the turnaround succeed than if you are planning and managing it.

There are drawbacks to working with a turnaround firm, however; the cost, for example. As this chapter already noted, the typical small business turnaround costs at least $50,000, which is higher than the cost of the average small business Chapter 11 bankruptcy.

Another drawback is that a turnaround firm may tell you things that you would rather not hear. For example, the firm may place at least some of the blame for your business's problems on you, your co-owners, your top managers, etc. Also, if you decide to work hand-in-hand with the firm, helping it carry out its turnaround activities and following its directives, you may be asked to do things that make you feel uncomfortable and may even upset you. For example, the firm may tell you that you must relinquish all or some of your management responsibilities to save your business.

> ### HOT TIP
>
> If you are unable to take the steps that the turnaround firm says are essential to saving your business, you can step aside during the turnaround process and someone else can fill your shoes— one of your co-owners, an employee, or someone who works for the turnaround firm. If you don't or won't cooperate with the turnaround firm, your board of directors may decide to re-place you, if your business is incorporated, or the turnaround firm may end its relationship with your business. At the very least, you will have wasted your business's precious money pay-ing for advice and expertise that you didn't heed.

Use a Turnaround Firm as Your Coach

If you opt to pursue this turnaround alternative, the turnaround firm will diagnose your business's problems and develop a plan for re-solving them. Then, it will be up to you to implement the plan, al-though the turnaround firm will be available to you on a limited basis for advice, information, encouragement, and feedback.

Lower cost is the main advantage of this alternative. However, if you are not well organized, are a poor manager, or are not willing to take decisive action as necessary, this option will be no more success-ful than the do-it-yourself "turnaround" option. Figure 3.1 highlights the personal qualities you need if you want to manage your business's turnaround, regardless of whether you manage it from start to finish or are in charge of the implementation phase only.

How to Find a Turnaround Firm for Your Business

Meet with several turnaround firms before you decide on one to hire. Your business's CPA, banker, or attorney, and possibly some of your close business associates, should be able to give you the names of rep-utable firms to consider. You may also want to check with business bank-

FIGURE 3.1
What It Takes to Manage a Turnaround

It takes special skills and abilities to manage your business's turnaround, whether you plan and manage it from beginning to end or take over after a turnaround firm has diagnosed its problems and prepared a plan of action for you. These include:

- *Good communication skills.* You will have to articulate clearly the root causes of your business's problems to your creditors, explain how a turnaround will address those problems, and make a convincing case for why the concessions your business needs from them are in their best interest, among other things. You will also have to communicate openly and honestly with your employees about the turnaround. For example, explain to them what a turnaround is and what your business hopes to accomplish with one, what they can expect during the turnaround process, how they may be affected by the turnaround, and what your business expects of them. If you are not able to convey this information effectively to your employees, their morale may suffer, which in turn will probably have a negative effect on productivity and the quality of their work and may also increase employee turnover. Each effect will impede the progress and success of your business's turnaround.

- *Motivational abilities.* Saving your business will almost certainly require sacrifice on the part of your employees. Among other things, they may have to accept pay cuts, forgo salary increases, move into smaller offices, do more with less, and so on. To keep them motivated under these circumstances, you must provide them with encouragement and support in ways that cost little or nothing.

- *Organizational skills.* Successfully implementing a turnaround plan, even with the help of a turnaround coach, can be a daunting organizational challenge. For example, at the same time that you are running your business, you must be able to juggle diverse turnaround-related responsibilities, direct and carry out multiple tasks, set realistic timetables, monitor the work of others, and respond to the questions of your creditors, suppliers, and employees, etc. If you can't keep your business on course and on schedule during the turnaround, the turnaround will fail and your business will be left with no choice but to file for bankruptcy.

ruptcy firms in your area, because they may also do turnarounds. If not, these bankruptcy firms can probably refer you to good turnaround firms. Another resource is the Turnaround Management Association located in Chicago. For a list of association members in your area, call the association at 312-578-6900, or go to its Web site at <www.turnaround.org>.

H O T   T I P

Hire a turnaround firm with specific experience working with businesses similar to yours that are in your same industry.

Once you have the names of several turnaround firms, set up a time to meet with each of them. The meetings will help you decide which firm you think will do the best job for your business. Base your decision on the following criteria:

- The philosophy of each firm toward turnarounds in general
- The specific approach that each firm suggests for the turnaround
- The amount of experience each firm has working with businesses similar to yours
- How much each firm will charge your business for handling the turnaround
- Your gut instinct regarding which firm will be best for your business

To help you arrive at a decision, here are some questions to ask during your getting-to-know-you meetings with each turnaround firm:

- Is my business a good candidate for a turnaround? Find out why or why not.
- In general terms, how will your firm help save my business?
- What factors are critical to the success of my business's turnaround?
- How quickly can your firm begin working with my business?
- About how long do you anticipate the turnaround will take?
- What are the potential stumbling blocks to a successful turnaround for my business, and how would your firm handle them?

- How does your firm charge for its services, and how much will it charge my business? Most turnaround firms will expect to receive an up-front retainer, or down payment, on the total cost of its services. The retainer is usually equivalent to one month of services.

H O T   T I P

Bring a pad of paper with you when you meet with each of the turnaround firms on your list. Use the pad to record their answers to your questions, as well as your impressions of each firm. Then, after you have met with all of the firms on your list, use the notes to refresh your memory of each firm and to compare their answers.

Turnaround firms will probably ask you questions, too, in order to help them make an initial assessment of your business's situation and determine whether or not a turnaround is feasible. Among other things, they may ask you about your business's revenues and expenses, the status of its debts, whether any of your business's secured creditors are threatening to take back their collateral, whether your business is behind on its payroll taxes, and so on.

Once you have decided on the turnaround firm to hire, don't pay any money until you have received an engagement letter from the firm or signed a more formally written contract with it. At a minimum, the engagement letter or contract should spell out the services the firm will provide to your business, the cost of its services and required terms of payment, and the duration of your agreement with one another.

What's Next?

Usually, there is no time to waste once a turnaround firm has been hired, so the firm will begin its work right away. Among other things, it will diagnose what is wrong with your business and why, assess your business's strengths and weaknesses, determine whether your business can become financially viable or needs to be liquidated, and if it can be turned around, what it will take to make it viable. Your business will be financially viable if it has the potential to become profitable once its debts are reorganized and the root causes of its problems are addressed. Without that potential, no business can expect to complete either a successful turnaround or a Chapter 11 bankruptcy. The "Playing Detective" section of this chapter discusses the diagnosis phase of the turnaround process.

WARNING

Sometimes, the cost of making a small business financially viable means that a turnaround is unrealistic.

Soon after the turnaround firm has been hired, it will meet with your business's lenders, other important creditors, and key suppliers. It will also meet with your business's employees, and if any of your employees are unionized, the firm will meet with representatives of their unions. The main purpose of these initial meetings will be to convince these various groups to give your business the time it needs to achieve a successful turnaround. The turnaround firm may ask for specific concessions from these various groups at some of these meetings, or it may set the stage for making those requests later.

At each of the meetings, the turnaround firm will introduce itself, explain how it intends to improve your business's finances, provide an overview of the turnaround process, and as appropriate, explain in either general or specific terms exactly what your business needs from each lender/creditor, supplier, employee, etc. Also, throughout the process, the firm will provide each of them with periodic reports regarding how your business's turnaround is proceeding.

The "Putting Out Fires" section of this chapter discusses the kinds of immediate concessions the turnaround firm is likely to ask from your business's lenders, creditors, and suppliers. The next section addresses issues related to your business's managers and employees in a turnaround.

Your Business's Managers and Employees

Early in the turnaround process, the turnaround firm will begin to assess the capabilities of your top managers, as well as their commitment to the turnaround. If it decides that a manager is not 100 percent behind the turnaround effort, or that a manager lacks the skills and knowledge your business needs to become profitable, the manager will be fired. If you are actively involved in the turnaround, you may be expected to do the firing. If you have handed over to the firm total control of your business's operations for the duration of the turnaround process, the turnaround firm will handle the firing.

> ### W A R N I N G
>
> It is commonplace in a turnaround for at least one high-profile manager to be fired very early in the process. The firing is a strategic move used by the turnaround firm to send a clear message to other employees that things are changing, and that if those employees do not get on board, their jobs will be in jeopardy, too. In some turnarounds, most, if not all, top management get the ax, because the turnaround firm views them as the people who are most responsible for the business's troubles and the ones most likely to resist the changes to come.

It is unlikely that your employees will abandon your firm in a mass exodus once they find out about the turnaround. Some employees will probably leave, however, especially if they suspect that they may be laid off at some point in the turnaround process. The turnaround firm may not replace the employees who leave, because losing them will help cut costs. At the same time, the turnaround firm will identify the employees who are essential to the success of your business's turnaround and future success, and it will probably offer them incentives to stay on. The incentives may include bonuses, salary increases, promises of future increases if your business achieves specific milestones during the turnaround process, promotions, and so on.

Playing Detective

One of the turnaround firm's very first steps will be to embark on a fact-finding mission in order to uncover clues that can help it determine exactly why your business is experiencing financial problems. It will complete its fact-finding as quickly as possible—probably in two weeks or less. Among other things, the turnaround firm will probably do the following to find clues:

- Review your business's financial data, including profit and loss statements, balance sheets, and cash flow statements.
- Examine your business's organizational structure and operations.
- Interview people who are familiar with your business, including you and any co-owners, your business's board of directors if your business is incorporated, and key managers.
- Interview some of your business's employees. The firm will randomly select the employees to be interviewed and will conduct the interviews on an anonymous basis to encourage candor. Your employees' take on why your business is in trouble may be quite different from your own, and therefore, their insights and information may be invaluable. They will probably be anxious to share their thoughts with the turnaround firm, either because they want your business to survive or because they welcome the opportunity to express the feelings of frustration and even anger they may feel toward your business. For many employees in a turnaround situation, being interviewed can provide an emotional catharsis.

The turnaround firm may also look outside your business for diagnostic information. For example, it may talk with your business's creditors and suppliers and maybe even with some of its customers.

HOT TIP

If you feel edgy or anxious about the employee interviews because you are worried about what they may say, remember why you hired the turnaround firm—to save your business. The interviews are a search for the truth, not a witch hunt.

The perspectives of outsiders regarding mistakes your business has made and what your business does right and wrong compared to its competitors, can be invaluable not only to diagnosing your business's problems but also to developing a plan to address them.

HOT TIP

When the turnaround firm contacts your business's customers, it will probably not tell them that your business is attempting a turnaround. Instead, it may explain that your business has hired it to do market research.

Putting Out Fires

Early in the process, the turnaround firm must begin addressing the problems that represent an immediate threat to your business, or there may be no business to turn around. A negative cash flow and angry, upset creditors usually represent the most immediate threats to a financially troubled business.

To generate a positive cash flow for your business, the turnaround firm will analyze how your business is spending its money and will look for expenses to slash and actions to take right away to free up money or generate additional income for your business. Among other things, the firm may sell off some of your business's assets, close down offices, lay off employees, improve your business's collections, revise credit policies, put a freeze on all travel and purchases over a certain dollar amount, and obtain bridge capital for your business. The turnaround firm will also tell your business how to spend its money.

Stay open to any and all expense reductions. Nothing in your business should be treated as a sacred cow, because if your business does not have enough cash flow to pay its debts, cover its operating expenses, and finance the cost of the turnaround, it cannot be saved.

Early in the turnaround process, the firm will have to deal with unsecured creditors who are angry and ready to take legal action to get the money your business owes to them. The firm must also deal with secured creditors who are preparing to take back their collateral, including assets that may be essential to the operation of your business. Your business's key suppliers may be threatening to tighten their terms of credit or cut off credit entirely to your business.

The turnaround firm will try to convince creditors and suppliers to hold off on doing anything that might cause additional damage to your business and make it even harder to accomplish a turnaround. For example, it may ask your business's lender not to cut off its line of credit or tighten the terms of that credit. It may ask key suppliers to continue working with your business on a COD basis. In addition, the turnaround firm may offer some of your business's secured creditors additional collateral (assuming your business has any unencumbered assets) and may ask other creditors for concessions that will help increase your business's cash flow.

Among other things, the turnaround firm may try to negotiate forbearance agreements with some creditors—agreements that restructure your business's debt in order to lower its costs either temporarily or permanently. For example, the firm may ask creditors to let your business make interest-only payments for a set period of time, extend the amount of time your business has to pay off its debts, or reduce the interest rates on the debts. The firm may also ask unsecured creditors to take less than the full amount your business owes to them as payment in full. Exactly how much will be a matter for negotiation between the turnaround firm and each creditor.

W A R N I N G

If your business gets additional time to pay off an existing debt, its monthly debt payments will be reduced but its total interest expense will increase.

Getting forbearance agreements and other concessions from your creditors and suppliers will probably take some negotiating. For example, they may ask your business for additional collateral or for a promise to make certain payments within a specific period of time, etc. However, they will be inclined to work with the turnaround firm if they believe:

- Your business's turnaround has a good chance of success.
- The concessions they are being asked to make are reasonable.
- They are more likely to get the money they are owed through a turnaround than if your business files for bankruptcy.

Also, creditors and suppliers are apt to give your business the concessions it needs if your business has been an important source of revenue for them in the past and they would like that revenue stream to continue. However, if they refuse to cooperate with your business, the turnaround firm may use the threat of bankruptcy to change their minds. That threat may work if they are worried that they won't get as much of what they are owed as they would in a turnaround and will probably have to wait longer to get paid. Also, they may want to avoid the legal fees they may have to pay if your business files for bankruptcy.

W A R N I N G

Your business's fully secured creditors may not be swayed by the threat of bankruptcy, because your business will have to pay them at least the value of their collateral if it files for bankruptcy.

In addition to slashing expenses and negotiating forbearance agreements and other concessions with creditors and suppliers, the turnaround firm may try to improve your business's cash flow by obtaining additional financing for it. If a traditional lender will not give your business that financing, the turnaround firm will probably contact lenders that regularly loan money to distressed businesses. However, loans from these lenders will come with a higher rate of interest than a traditional loan. And, your business will probably have to secure the loans with collateral.

The Turnaround Plan

Once the turnaround firm has a good grasp of why your business is in trouble and has a sense of how cooperative your creditors and suppliers will be and what may be the major stumbling blocks to your business's turnaround, it will draft a turnaround plan. This plan is a strategic document that describes how your business's resources—cash, assets, and people—will be leveraged in order to solve its problems, give it permanent stability, and make it profitable. Most turnaround plans address both financial and operational issues.

During the drafting process, the turnaround firm will contact your business's key creditors and suppliers to get their feedback on the plan's details and will make changes to the plan as necessary and appropriate based on that input. This give-and-take is critical to the success of your business's turnaround. For example, some creditors may withhold support of the plan unless it is revised in specific ways. Assuming the changes they insist on are reasonable from your business's perspective, the draft plan will probably be revised accordingly. However, if the turnaround firm is unable to reach an agreement with one of your business's more important creditors—a secured creditor or a primary supplier that you owe a lot of money to, for example—your business may end up having to file for bankruptcy.

Every business is different, so the details of a turnaround plan vary from business to business. However, most turnaround plans call for certain actions more often than not, including:

- Fire or lay off nonessential employees and managers.
- Reduce employee salaries and/or delay salary increases.
- Reassign employees to different jobs.
- Retrain employees for new jobs or so they can perform their current jobs more effectively.
- Hire new employees who have the expertise and experience to help a business grow and prosper.
- Take specific steps to improve productivity.

HOT TIP

Consider outsourcing the payroll-related aspects of your business's bookkeeping to save money and ensure that your business complies with its payroll tax obligations. Many accounting firms offer this service. They will calculate deductions and employee pay, generate checks, and take care of payroll taxes.

- Sell unneeded assets.
- Sell old inventory. There are firms that will pay cash for a business's outdated or slow-moving inventory.
- Sell fixed assets to a leasing company and then rent them back from the company. Many commercial banks and commercial finance companies have leasing divisions. This arrangement is most often an option for firms that own vehicles, equipment, and buildings.
- Eliminate products and services that do not make money or are not part of the business.
- Reprice products and services.
- Generate new or stronger revenue streams by repackaging or repositioning products and services.
- Add to the business's product-and-service mix.
- Lease out excess capacity.
- Move to less expensive office space. This option makes sense if a lease is about to run out, or if the financial consequences of breaking the lease are less than the savings a business will realize from moving.
- Revamp credit and collections policies and procedures.
- Improve sales and marketing.
- Renegotiate the business's relationships with key suppliers.
- Obtain new financing if necessary.

To obtain additional cash for your business, the turnaround plan may call for obtaining a line of credit against its receivables with a commercial finance company or for working with a *factor*. A factor is a company that purchases other company's receivables. If your business has a lot of past-due receivables, the factor may be willing to buy them, and although your business will not realize big bucks from the sale, getting at least something on old receivables is better than getting no money at all.

Once the Turnaround Plan Is in Place

Once your business has a turnaround plan that is acceptable to its key creditors and suppliers, the plan implementation phase will begin. During this phase, those creditors and suppliers will watch your business carefully to make sure that all of the changes and improvements spelled out in its plan are carried out, and that your business's financial situation begins to improve as the turnaround firm promised it would. However, once the implementation phase is underway, it is possible that your business's turnaround plan will have to be revised. Assuming that the changes the turnaround firm wants to make are not substantial and do not harm your business's creditors and suppliers, the implementation phase will probably proceed forward. However, if any creditors or suppliers balk at the changes or if it appears your business cannot be turned around after all, your business may be left with no option but to file for either a Chapter 11 or a Chapter 7 bankruptcy. Which type of bankruptcy will depend on whether you still want to try to save your business, whether your business can finance a reorganization bankruptcy, and the attitude of your business's creditors and suppliers toward your business, among other things.

4

Bankruptcy Basics

Bankruptcy is a legal process, governed by federal bankruptcy law, that can help financially troubled businesses when they cannot afford to pay what they owe. If your business is considering bankruptcy, it has two options: a Chapter 11 reorganization or a Chapter 7 liquidation. Although both types of bankruptcy are available to any form of business regardless of its legal structure, this book is written for small, closely held corporations. However, this chapter and the next two chapters in this book provide a limited amount of bankruptcy-related information for sole proprietorships, because many of the rules of bankruptcy are different for that kind of business.

Filing a Chapter 11 bankruptcy gives your business an opportunity to reorganize its debts and pay as much of what it owes as possible under the protection of the federal bankruptcy court, so that it can continue to operate. During the time that your business is in bankruptcy, it can also begin to implement other changes that may be necessary to make it profitable. Ideally, at the completion of the bankruptcy, your business will be stronger and more economically viable than it was at the start.

On the other hand, filing for Chapter 7 will spell the end of your business. Your business will have to stop operating as soon as it files for bankruptcy, and a bankruptcy trustee will take title to its assets. Later, the trustee will sell those assets and use the sale proceeds to pay as much of your business's debt as possible.

This chapter provides an overview of both types of bankruptcies. It:

- Offers important prebankruptcy planning advice.
- Explains the importance of working with a bankruptcy attorney and tells you how to find a good one.
- Tells you how to initiate a bankruptcy and what will happen immediately after you do.
- Highlights the roles of the key players in a bankruptcy—you, as the owner of the business; your business's creditors; the bankruptcy trustee; and the bankruptcy judge.
- Explains the priority of debts in a bankruptcy according to federal bankruptcy law.

Chapters 5 and 6 provide more detailed information on the Chapters 11 and 7 bankruptcy processes.

Reap the Most Benefits by Planning Ahead

Planning for bankruptcy with the help of a bankruptcy attorney will help position your business to get rid of the maximum amount of debt. It will also help you minimize the potential impact of the bankruptcy on your personal finances, if that is a concern for you.

Ideally, you should begin planning your business's bankruptcy 6 to 12 months before your business will actually file. Unfortunately, however, most small business owners don't consult with a bankruptcy attorney until they are in a crisis, which means they have little or no time for prebankruptcy planning. For example:

- Their business is out of cash.
- A creditor is about to take back one of the assets their business needs to keep operating.
- Their business is about to be evicted from the space it is renting or its mortgage lender is threatening foreclosure.
- The IRS is threatening to shut down their business.

Prebankruptcy planning is especially important if you want to use Chapter 11 to save your business, because achieving that goal will depend in large part on whether your business has enough cash to continue operating throughout the bankruptcy process and also pay for the bankruptcy. If your business is like most financially troubled businesses, amassing such a "war chest" of cash will not happen overnight.

H O T   T I P

It is always advisable to plan for the possibility of bankruptcy when you are just beginning your business. Among other things, your planning should include taking steps to help protect your personal assets from the repercussions of bankruptcy. If you try to protect those assets too close to the start of a bankruptcy, the bankruptcy court may accuse you of fraud.

When you meet with a bankruptcy attorney during the prebankruptcy planning process, the attorney will provide you with this kind of advice:

- If you want to try to save your business through Chapter 11, do not return to your business's secured creditors any assets that are essential to its continued operation. The attorney will explain that your business may be able to keep those assets by making *adequate protection payments* to its creditors during the bankruptcy process. Adequate protection payments are discussed in Chapter 5.
- Do not pay one creditor at the expense of other creditors during the 90 days preceding the date your business files its bankruptcy petition. (Filing the petition marks the start of a bankruptcy.) In bankruptcy parlance, this kind of payment is referred to as a *preferential payment.* Such a prohibition applies to both Chapter 7 and Chapter 11 bankruptcies. If your business makes a preferential payment prior to filing for Chapter 7, the bankruptcy trustee will try to get the money back so that he or she can distribute those funds among your business's creditors according to the priorities set out in federal bankruptcy law. The "Some Debts Are More Important Than Others" section later in this chapter explains those priorities. If your business makes a preferential payment prior to beginning a Chapter 11 bankruptcy, some of your business's creditors may file motions with the court asking that the payment be reversed.
- Do not transfer any of your business's assets into the name of an individual or another business during the year prior to the start

of a Chapter 7 bankruptcy. If the court finds out that your business made such a transfer, the transfer may be treated as *fraudulent*. If it is, the court will reverse the transfer, so that the asset can be liquidated and the funds can be distributed to your business's creditors according to their priority in federal bankruptcy law.

WARNING

During the year prior to the start of its bankruptcy, if your business reimburses you for money you loaned to it, the reimbursement may be considered a *preferential payment*. If it is, you will have to return the money to the court.

- If you are running your business as a sole proprietorship, do not get a cash advance of more than $1,150 during the 60 days preceding the start of a Chapter 7 bankruptcy. If you do, that debt may not be wiped out through bankruptcy, and it will be your personal responsibility to pay the debt after the bankruptcy is over. The same prohibition applies to purchases of more than $1,150 worth of luxury items or services from a single creditor that you make with a credit card up to 60 days prior to filing for bankruptcy.

WARNING

Do not pay for any goods and services with a postdated check. If the check bounces and your business cannot make good on it, you may be criminally prosecuted for passing a bad check. Bankruptcy offers no protection from bad check–related fines and penalties.

How to Find a Bankruptcy Attorney to Represent Your Business

Don't even think about trying to handle your own business bankruptcy! Bankruptcy is a complicated legal process, and your business cannot fully benefit from it without the help of an experienced bankruptcy attorney. Working with an attorney is especially important if you want your business to file for Chapter 11, because that particular bankruptcy process is quite complicated and is fraught with potential problems for a business.

> ## W A R N I N G
>
> You are legally prohibited from acting as your business's own attorney if your business is incorporated. Nonlawyers cannot represent individuals in legal proceedings, and in the eyes of the law, a corporation is equivalent to an individual.

The best way to find a good business bankruptcy attorney is to interview several qualified attorneys and then make your pick. To get the names of attorneys to interview, you may want to contact:

- Your business associates. Some of them may have filed bankruptcy in the past and were happy with the attorneys they used.
- Your business's CPA, company attorney, or another attorney you know and respect.
- Your local, county, or state bar association. Bar associations often maintain lawyer referral services. However, a bar association referral is not equivalent to a recommendation.
- The turnaround firm your business may be working with. Many firms have their own bankruptcy attorneys on staff or have business relationships with bankruptcy attorneys.
- The American Board of Certification at <www.abcworld.org>. This organization certifies attorneys in both business and consumer bankruptcy law.

The U.S. bankruptcy trustee with the federal district bankruptcy court in your area may be another source of attorney names. Although

> ### W A R N I N G
>
> Don't ask your business's suppliers or creditors for referrals to a good bankruptcy attorney. Although they may suspect that your business is having financial problems, there is no point in signaling your plans to them any sooner than you have to. Also, it's usually not a good idea to ask your customers or clients for referrals, because they may be less inclined to work with you once they know that your business is having financial problems. Plus, they may share their information with others.

the trustee will not tell you which attorney to hire, he or she regularly observes bankruptcy attorneys in action and knows who the good ones are.

Once You Have Some Attorney Names

Once you have the names of three or four reputable bankruptcy attorneys, call them to schedule initial consultations. You will probably not be charged for these meetings, but to make certain, ask if there will be a charge when you call to schedule your appointments. An initial consultation gives you the chance to ask about an attorney's experience, find out how the attorney charges for his or her services, and assess which attorney will do the best job for your business.

Here are some of the things you should find out during each initial consultation:

- How long has the attorney been practicing bankruptcy law, and how many cases similar to yours has he or she handled? You want an attorney who has specific experience working with businesses like yours in terms of annual revenues, size, type of business, and industry. This is particularly important if you plan to file a Chapter 11 bankruptcy. Also, be sure to find out how many cases the attorney has *personally* handled, rather than the number of cases his or her law firm has handled.
- What issues will your business face during its bankruptcy, and what options will it have for dealing with them?

H O T   T I P

Attorneys in some states can become board-certified in bank-ruptcy law, which means that they have a particular interest in that type of law. In fact, a board-certified bankruptcy attorney may only handle bankruptcy cases. After obtaining his or her law license, an attorney must take additional courses in bankruptcy law and must pass a state exam to become board-certified. The attorney must also take bankruptcy classes each year to main-tain the certification.

• How will the attorney charge for his or her services? If your business files for Chapter 11, the attorney will expect to be paid a substantial up-front retainer, or down payment, on the total cost of the bankruptcy. The amount of the retainer will be based on the attorney's hourly rate—most bankruptcy attor-neys charge between $125 and $350 per hour—and on the number of hours that he or she anticipates spending on your business's bankruptcy case, from beginning to end. Even a run-of-the-mill Chapter 11 is apt to cost between $10,000 and $25,000 for a mom-and-pop operation—a business with no more than 15 employees, no more than 15 creditors, and $500,000 or less in debt. A larger small business can expect to pay between $30,000 and $50,000 for its Chapter 11. However, both figures could skyrocket if the bankruptcy involves a lot of court motions and hearings. Extremely complicated Chapter 11s that last for many months or even years and involve nu-merous court hearings and protracted negotiations with credi-tors will cost much, much more.

In addition to the attorney's fee, you will also have to reimburse your business's attorney for all of the bankruptcy-related expenses he or she incurs on its behalf. These expenses will include court costs, copying, postage, and delivery services, among other things.

A Chapter 7 bankruptcy tends to be more predictable and less complicated than a Chapter 11. Therefore, if your business is going to file for Chapter 7, you may be able to find a bankruptcy attorney who will charge a flat fee for legal services rather than billing by the hour. The attorney's fee will probably range between $1,500 and $3,500, plus expenses.

There are other factors besides the type of bankruptcy that will affect how much your business pays a bankruptcy attorney. These other factors include:

- Whether the attorney is practicing law in a large metropolitan area or a less populated or rural community. Lawyers in large urban areas like New York City and Los Angeles tend to charge more than lawyers in Peoria, Illinois, or Tucson, Arizona, for example.
- The size of the firm the attorney works for. As a rule, attorneys with large firms charge more than attorneys with small firms. Among other reasons, their overhead expenses tend to be higher.
- The number of years that the attorney has been practicing law. Experienced attorneys tend to charge more than attorneys with less experience.
- The complexity of the bankruptcy, if your business is going to file for Chapter 11. Its complexity will depend on the number, type, and value of your business's assets; whether your business's creditors are hostile toward the bankruptcy; and so on.

Other Factors to Consider When You Are in the Market for a Business Bankruptcy Attorney

You may never have had to deal with the legal system before, much less go through a bankruptcy, so it is likely that you are feeling a lot of anxiety and trepidation about the process. However, an attorney who is willing to explain the bankruptcy process to you using words you can understand—not legalese—and who provides clear answers to your questions can help make you feel less anxious and worried. Therefore, if any of the attorneys you meet with use legal mumbo-jumbo, ignore your questions, or act as though your questions are bothersome, think twice before you hire him or her to represent your business.

If you want to save your business through Chapter 11, it is also important to consider the negotiation and courtroom skills of the attorneys you meet with. Their ability to negotiate with your business's creditors and suppliers during the bankruptcy process, think on their feet, and argue persuasively can make the difference between a successful reorganization and one that ends up having to be converted to a Chapter 7 liquidation. Furthermore, an attorney with these qualities is better able to keep your business's bankruptcy moving forward, which will help minimize the total cost.

There are a couple ways to assess the negotiation and courtroom skills of the attorneys you meet with. For example, you can ask other attorneys you may know about the attorneys' reputations, and you can observe the attorneys in action in the courtroom. Most courtroom proceedings are open to the public, so you can walk into a courtroom, watch, and listen, no questions asked.

HOT TIP

Judges like to consider themselves impartial decision makers. The truth is, however, they are human beings like everyone else. Sometimes, therefore, a judge's decision is influenced by his or her rapport with an attorney or by an attorney's reputation.

In the end, you should base your decision about which bankruptcy attorney to hire on the reputations of the attorneys you meet with, their understanding of your business's financial situation, their responsiveness to your questions and concerns, their hourly rates, and your own gut instinct regarding which one will do the best job for your business. Bottom line: Hire the very best bankruptcy attorney your business can afford.

What Kind of Bankruptcy Should Your Business File?

The bankruptcy attorney you decide to hire will help you determine the most appropriate type of bankruptcy for your business, taking into account your goals for the business—keep it going or shut it down—as well as your business's financial condition and relationship to creditors and suppliers. For example, if key creditors are extremely hostile toward your business, or if your business owes too much money relative to your business's ability to pay them, the attorney will probably advise that your business file for Chapter 7, even if you hoped that you would be able to save it through a Chapter 11.

Chapter 11 is a realistic option for your business if:

- There is a strong likelihood that your business can become profitable if it has time to reorganize its debts under the protection of the bankruptcy court and make appropriate changes in its operations, staffing, etc.
- Your business continues to enjoy relatively good relationships with its creditors despite its financial problems.
- Your business is concerned that some of its secured creditors are about to take back their collateral and/or that the IRS is going to try to collect on its past-due taxes.
- You appreciate what it will take to make your business profitable.
- Your business has the resources—expertise and money—to reorganize.
- Your business's cash and credit positions are relatively strong.

WARNING

Don't count on an economic upturn to make your business profitable. Becoming profitable will take a lot of hard work on your part and on the part of your management team and key employees.

The attorney will advise that your business file for Chapter 7 if:

- Its chances of becoming profitable are slim to none.
- Your business cannot afford to pay its debts. Chapter 7 is especially appropriate if your business has a lot of secured debt.
- Your business does not have enough time to build up the cash reserves it needs to fund its operations during a Chapter 11 bankruptcy, or it does not have the ability to build that "war chest" given the state of its finances and relationships with creditors.
- Your business cannot afford the cost of a Chapter 11.

> ## WARNING
>
> If your business files for Chapter 11, its bankruptcy attorney will prepare a written reorganization plan for the business. Before your business can get out of bankruptcy, a majority of its creditors must approve the plan. Getting creditor approval can be an uphill battle for many businesses. In fact, a high percentage of small businesses cannot get that approval or run out of funds before their plans are approved and have to convert their Chapter 11s to Chapter 7s as a result.

Beginning a Bankruptcy

Every bankruptcy, regardless of whether it is a Chapter 11 or a Chapter 7, starts the same way—with the filing of a *Petition for Relief* with the bankruptcy court. When your business files its petition, it must also pay a filing fee, the amount of which depends on the type of bankruptcy. Although those fees change periodically, presently they are:

- $835 for a Chapter 11
- $200 for a Chapter 7

Your business's bankruptcy attorney will complete the petition paperwork and pay the filing fee. He or she will also complete and file a number of other documents with the court. To prepare them, the attorney will need copies of your business's profit-and-loss statements and balance sheets for the past two years; your business tax returns for the past three years; copies of your business's unexpired contracts, including leases; and your business's insurance binders, among other things.

The other documents the attorney will file include:

- Detailed schedules, or lists, of your business's debts and assets. The debt schedules will indicate the name and address of each of your business's creditors, the balance on each of your business's outstanding debts, and the date that your business incurred each debt. If any of the debts are secured, the schedules will also describe the assets that secure, or collateralize, those debts, and will indicate a market value for each of the assets. An asset's market value is what the asset is worth now, not what your business paid for it.

- A *statement of affairs.* This statement provides information about your business's books and records, income, financial statements, and assets, among other things. It also indicates whether your business has been sued recently or lost any of its assets in a repossession or foreclosure. In addition, the statement of affairs indicates whether your business made any preferential payments to its creditors during the 90 days prior to the start of its bankruptcy or transferred any assets out of its own name during the year prior to filing.

W A R N I N G

Be sure that you provide your business's attorney with complete and accurate information about *all* of your business's debts, including the amount of each debt and an accurate address for each creditor. This is important because only the debts that are listed on your business's schedules will be included in its bankruptcy.

If your business files for Chapter 11, the attorney will submit two other documents to the court: a disclosure statement and a reorganization plan. However, the attorney will have 120 days after the start of your business's bankruptcy to file each of these documents. Chapter 5 provides detailed information about disclosure statements and reorganization plans.

Figure 4.1 provides a comprehensive list of the various documents your business may have to file during its bankruptcy. Appendixes A and B include samples of many of the documents.

Your Business's Bankruptcy Estate

The assets listed on your business's schedules of assets are collectively referred to as its *bankruptcy estate.* To be accurate and complete, the schedules should include any asset that your business owns or has a financial interest in, including:

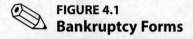
FIGURE 4.1
Bankruptcy Forms

This figure lists various bankruptcy documents that are filed with the court. A bankruptcy petition, a statement of financial affairs, and schedules of assets and debts are filed in every bankruptcy, although the specific schedules your business files will depend on the nature of its assets—real or personal property—and on the nature of its debts—secured or unsecured debt. However, some of the documents on this list apply only to either a Chapter 11 or a Chapter 7 bankruptcy. For example, *disclosure statements* are only filed in Chapter 11 bankruptcies. Appendixes A and B include sample bankruptcy forms:

- The bankruptcy petition

- *Statement of Financial Affairs*

- Summary of Schedules

- Schedule A, *Real Property*. Real property is real estate.

- Schedule B, *Personal Property*. All assets other than real estate.

- Schedule C, *Property Claimed as Exempt*. This form is only filed in a personal bankruptcy. Therefore, it would be filed if your business is run as a sole proprietorship.

- Schedule D, *Creditors Holding Secured Claims*

- Schedule E, *Creditors Holding Unsecured Priority Claims*

- Schedule F, *Creditors Holding Unsecured Nonpriority Claims*

- Schedule G, *Executory Contracts and Unexpired Leases*

- Schedule H, *Codebtors*

- *Declaration Concerning Debtor's Schedules*

- *Creditor Mailing List*

- *Disclosure Statement*. This form is only filed in a Chapter 11 bankruptcy and is created by the attorney for the debtor.

- *Reorganization plan*. This is only filed in a Chapter 11 bankruptcy and is created by the attorney for the debtor.

- *Initial Debtor's Report*. This report only applies to businesses that file for Chapter 11. It must be filed within 30 days of the start of a bankruptcy. The report describes your business, provides a 90-day projection of your business's income and expenses, and helps prove that your business has adequate resources to complete a Chapter 11, among other things.

- Any asset that the trustee takes back or recovers after your business's bankruptcy begins because of an illegal transfer, a preferential payment, and so on
- All of the profits, proceeds, and other income generated by the assets in your business's bankruptcy estate while it is in bankruptcy

Exempting Assets from Your Bankruptcy Estate When You File a Personal Bankruptcy

If your financially troubled business is a sole proprietorship, and you decide that filing for bankruptcy is the best way to deal with its debts, your business will not file for bankruptcy. Instead, you will file for *personal bankruptcy,* because in the eyes of the law, there is no difference between you and your business—you are one and the same. In other words, your business debts are your personal debts, and your business assets are your personal assets. Therefore, your bankruptcy estate will include the assets you use in your personal life as well as the ones you use in your business.

When you file a personal bankruptcy, regardless of whether you file a Chapter 11 or a Chapter 7, you are entitled to exempt certain assets, up to a specific dollar amount, from the bankruptcy, even though you must include them on your asset schedules. You get to keep those assets. Only your nonexempt assets—the ones you do not exempt—will be part of the bankruptcy. This means that you may be able to continue your business, even if you file for Chapter 7, if the assets you exempt are the ones you need to run it.

Each state has its own law that spells out the specific types of assets you can exempt. Federal bankruptcy law also provides a list of exemptions. In a few states, you can chose whether you want to use your state's exemptions or the federal ones. However, in most states, you must use the federal exemptions.

HOT TIP

State exemptions tend to be more generous than federal exemptions. Florida and Texas offer especially generous exemptions.

After you decide which assets you want to exempt, your creditors will have 30 days from the date of your first creditors meeting to object to any of the exemptions. If a creditor files an objection, the bankruptcy judge will schedule a hearing, and at the end of the hearing, the judge will rule on the objection. However, your business's attorney can try to resolve creditor objections prior to the hearing. The creditors meeting will be discussed later in this chapter.

The Key Players in a Business Bankruptcy

Understanding the role of the various players in your business's bankruptcy and the interests that they have in the bankruptcy helps you understand the bankruptcy process. There are four key players in your business's bankruptcy:

1. You, as your business's owner, and any co-owners you may have
2. Your business's creditors
3. The bankruptcy trustee
4. The bankruptcy judge

The interests of one player may conflict with the interests of another player during your business's bankruptcy, and the conflicts may create delays and expenses for your business. Therefore, in a Chapter 11 bankruptcy, balancing the interests of the various players in your business's bankruptcy can be strategically important to its success.

You, as the Owner of Your Business, and Any Co-Owners

As the owner of your business, you will be responsible for providing the bankruptcy attorney with the information he or she needs to complete all of the bankruptcy paperwork and represent your business throughout the bankruptcy process. This is true whether your business files for Chapter 11 or Chapter 7. However, if your business files for Chapter 11, you will also be involved in helping the attorney draft a reorganization plan for your business and for running the business according to the rules of federal bankruptcy law.

Your Business's Creditors

Like most business bankruptcies, there will probably be two basic types of creditors involved in yours—secured and unsecured creditors. A *secured creditor* is a creditor that has a lien on one of your business's assets. That asset is its *collateral.* If your business falls behind on its payments to a secured creditor, the creditor is legally entitled to take back that collateral. Common examples of secured debts include bank loans that are collateralized by real estate, equipment, machinery, or accounts receivables.

The loss of an important asset can be devastating to a business. Therefore, it is not uncommon for a small business to file for bankruptcy as soon as it has reason to believe that a secured creditor is about to take back its collateral. Although the business may lose that asset anyway, the court will issue an *automatic stay* as soon as the business has filed. The automatic stay will put a temporary halt to all creditor collection actions in order to give the business time to figure out what to do about its debts. The next section of this chapter provides additional information about the automatic stay.

An *unsecured creditor* is a creditor that does not have a lien on any of your business's assets. Common examples of unsecured creditors include suppliers, credit card companies, utilities, phone companies, and professionals, such as CPAs and attorneys.

The Bankruptcy Trustee

The trustee's responsibilities in your business's bankruptcy will depend on the type of bankruptcy your business files. For example, in a Chapter 7 bankruptcy, the court will appoint a private trustee— usually an attorney or an accountant—to take control of your business's assets, liquidate them, and distribute the sale proceeds to your business's creditors.

In a Chapter 11 bankruptcy, however, the trustee will be a federal employee who functions independently of the bankruptcy court, and who will not be involved in the day-to-day details of running your business. Instead, your business will be a *debtor in possession* during its bankruptcy, which means that it will remain in control of its own affairs unless the court decides it is not following the rules of bankruptcy or is not acting in the best interest of its creditors. Therefore, the trustee's primary responsibility will be to ensure that your business abides by all of the federal rules that apply to Chapter 11 and does not squander any of the assets that it could use to pay its debts. The trustee will also call and preside over your business's creditors meetings and will tell the bankruptcy judge whether or not he or she thinks the judge should approve your business's reorganization plan.

The Bankruptcy Judge

Throughout your business's bankruptcy, a federal bankruptcy judge will preside over court hearings and will rule on any motions filed by your business or by its creditors, after there has been a hearing on that motion. Motions are more apt to be filed in a Chapter 11 bankruptcy than in a Chapter 7.

In addition, in a Chapter 11 bankruptcy, the judge will have the final say on whether your business's reorganization plan gets approved, after your business's creditors vote for or against the plan. More often than not, if a majority of creditors approve the plan, the judge will, too. Once he or she does, your business's bankruptcy is over.

The Automatic Stay

After your business has filed its bankruptcy petition, the court will initiate an *automatic stay*, which is a court injunction stopping most, but not all, creditor collection actions. It also halts any collection-related lawsuits filed against your business, prohibits creditors from trying to

---

H O T   T I P

The court will notify creditors about the *automatic stay*. However, because it will take a while for the court to do that, your bankruptcy attorney will contact each of your business's creditors right away to let them know that an automatic stay has been invoked.

enforce judgments against your business, and bars creditors from proceeding with foreclosures and repossessions. If your business is a sole proprietorship and you have filed a personal bankruptcy, the automatic stay also prevents your wages from being garnished while you are in bankruptcy. The automatic stay will remain in effect until your business has completed its bankruptcy or until the court dismisses the bankruptcy.

As helpful as the automatic stay is, there are things that it does not stop. For example, it does not put a temporary halt to:

- IRS audits and requests for information regarding a possible tax deficiency. However, if the IRS decides as a result of its actions that your business owes it money, and you have filed a Chapter 7 bankruptcy, the agency must wait to collect on that debt until your business's bankruptcy is over. The same is true if you personally owe the IRS money.
- Any criminal actions that have been filed against you. Usually, this only applies to personal bankruptcies.

During the bankruptcy process, one of your business's secured creditors may file a *motion to lift the automatic stay* in order to get the court's permission to take back its collateral. The court will schedule a hearing on the motion. Most likely, if your business needs the collateral to reorganize, the judge will allow your business to keep it. However, as a condition of allowing your business to continue benefiting from the asset, the judge will probably order your business to make monthly *adequate protection payments* to the creditor that filed the motion. Your business will have to make those payments as long as it is in bankruptcy.

Other Aspects of the Automatic Stay

An automatic stay also protects your business from losing its utility service when it owes the utility money. However, the automatic stay *does not* prevent the utility from demanding that your business pay a "reasonable deposit" for continued utility service, assuming that your business did not pay one when it initiated the service. "Reasonable" is usually considered to be equal to the average cost of two months of utility service for a business. To be enforceable, the utility company must demand a "reasonable deposit," in writing, within 20 days of the start of your business's bankruptcy.

Also, if your landlord initiated an eviction prior to the start of the automatic stay, your business can remain in the space it is renting as long as it gets caught up on its past-due rent. However, your business may have just a few days to come up with that money, and if it can't, your landlord can proceed with the eviction after getting permission from the bankruptcy court.

Creditor Proof of Claim Forms

After your business's bankruptcy has begun, its secured and unsecured creditors will file *proof of claim* forms with the bankruptcy court. They must file their claims by a *bar date,* which the judge will set. If your business has filed for Chapter 7, any creditor claims that are not filed by this date will not be paid from the distribution of your business's *liquidated assets,* assuming there is any money to distribute.

If your business has filed for Chapter 11 and a creditor does not file a claim by the bar date, your business's bankruptcy attorney can file a *motion to bar the claim.* After the motion has been filed, the creditor with the claim that is the subject of the motion will have 20 days to file a *response.* Whether a response is filed or not, there will be a hearing on your business's motion at the end of the 20-day period. If no response is filed, the bankruptcy judge will probably rule that your business does not have to pay that debt, and the court will discharge it. If the creditor does file a response by the deadline, after holding a hearing during which the judge will listen to arguments from your business's attorney and from the creditor's attorney, the judge will decide whether or not your business must address the debt in its plan of reorganization.

Your business can object to any of the claims that its creditors file. It may object to a claim in order to eliminate that debt from its bankruptcy, reduce the amount of the debt, or, if your business has filed for Chapter 11, lower the priority of the debt. The section "In Bankruptcy, Some Debts Are More Important Than Others" later in this chapter explains how federal bankruptcy law prioritizes debts.

Whenever your business files an objection to a creditor's claim, the court will notify the creditor and will schedule a hearing to consider the objection. After listening to arguments from both sides of the issue, the judge will rule on your business's objection.

The Initial Debtor's Conference

In a Chapter 11 bankruptcy, an *initial debtor's conference* will be scheduled for sometime during the 30 to 40 days following the date your business's bankruptcy petition is filed. Your business's bankruptcy attorney, the bankruptcy trustee, and you will participate in this meeting.

The main purpose of the initial debtor's conference is to make sure that your business's asset and debt schedules are complete and accurate. After the trustee reviews the schedules, he or she may require that the attorney amend some of them. The trustee will also want to make certain that your business has opened up a new bank account as a *debtor in possession.* Your business must use this account throughout its bankruptcy.

The Creditors Meeting

About a month after your business's Chapter 7 bankruptcy has begun and about two months after the start of your business's Chapter 11 bankruptcy, a *creditors meeting,* also called a *341 meeting,* will take place. The meeting will be run by the trustee assigned to the bankruptcy or by someone else with the bankruptcy court.

This meeting represents your business's first formal meeting with its creditors since the start of its bankruptcy. Any creditor can attend, but your business's secured creditors are most apt to show up, because they may be anxious to find out what is going to happen to their collateral.

You must attend the meeting as owner of your business, but your business's bankruptcy attorney will attend too. If you do not attend the meeting, the judge will probably dismiss the bankruptcy. If it is dismissed, your business will not be protected by the automatic stay anymore, so its assets will be fair game for creditors.

H O T   T I P

Let your business's bankruptcy attorney know if you cannot attend the creditors meeting on the date that it is scheduled. The attorney will ask the court to change the meeting date.

During the creditors meeting, the trustee will ask you questions to help make sure that your business's schedules are complete and accurate. If your business has filed for Chapter 11, the trustee will also confirm that you understand your responsibilities while your business is a *debtor in possession.* For example, your business must prepare and file monthly financial reports with the trustee and pay him or her a quarterly fee as well. The trustee will also want to know why you think that your business can reorganize successfully.

If your business has filed for Chapter 11, the creditors who attend the meeting may also ask you questions to help them assess the state of your business's finances, how much they may receive from your business, and how likely it is that your business's reorganization will be successful. Your business's secured creditors will also want to know what your business intends to do with their collateral.

In Bankruptcy, Some Debts Are More Important Than Others

Federal bankruptcy law classifies debts according to their priority or importance. Therefore, regardless of what kind of bankruptcy your business files, the law says that some debts are more important than others. If your business does not have sufficient funds to pay all of its debts, it must pay its highest-priority debts first.

The priority of debts begins with the most important debt and ends with the least important debt, according to bankruptcy law:

- *Super priority claims.* In a Chapter 11, these claims represent the money your business may owe to creditors that loaned it money after its bankruptcy began.
- *Administrative claims.* The fees and expenses of your business's bankruptcy attorney are treated as administrative expenses. Also, the fees and expenses of any professionals the attorney or bankruptcy trustee may hire to help with your business's bankruptcy are administrative expenses. These professionals often include CPAs and appraisers, among others. Other administrative claims may include money that your business owes to a vendor that sells it goods or services while it is in bankruptcy and the trustee's fees and expenses. The trustee's fees and expenses are highest in a Chapter 7 bankruptcy, because compared to the responsibilities of the trustee in a Chapter 11, the trustee has many more responsibilities. For example, in a Chapter 7 bankruptcy,

the trustee must identify your business's assets, determine their value, take title to them, liquidate them, and distribute the sale proceeds to your business's creditors.

- *Claims for certain deposits given to your business for future services, products, or leases that it has not yet provided or delivered on.* According to bankruptcy law, there is a maximum of $900 per claim.
- *Secured debts.* Your business must pay the full market value of the assets that collateralize each of its secured debts in a Chapter 11.
- *Priority debts.* These include:
  - All valid claims for unpaid wages that were earned by your business's employees during the 90-day period prior to the start of its bankruptcy. There is a $4,650 per employee limit for each claim.
  - All valid claims for contributions to your business's employee benefits plan—up to a maximum of $4,650 per employee—related to the work each employee performed for your business no more than 180 days prior to the date of its bankruptcy.
  - Most of your business's unpaid taxes as well as any tax-related penalties that are past due for the three years prior to the start of its bankruptcy.
  - Any money that your business may have withheld from its employees' paychecks for Social Security, taxes, and so on, but spent for some other purposes.
- *General unsecured debts.* In many bankruptcies, general unsecured creditors end up with just cents on the dollar.

In a Chapter 7 bankruptcy, the trustee will pay your business's debts in the order of their priority, paying the highest-priority debts first. If the trustee does not have enough money to pay lower-priority debts, the court will discharge most of them. However, after your business's bankruptcy is complete, if you personally guaranteed any of the debts that were not paid during the bankruptcy, your business's creditors can come after your personal assets to collect what they are owed. The IRS can also go after your personal assets to collect any past-due payroll taxes that did not get paid during your business's bankruptcy.

In a Chapter 11 bankruptcy, your business's reorganization plan will probably provide for the concurrent payment of debts with different priorities. However, if your business cannot afford to pay all of its debts, it must pay the highest-priority debts first. In many Chapter 11 bankruptcies, unsecured creditors receive just a fraction of the money they are owed.

WARNING

If your business is incorporated and you have co-owners, the IRS can come after the personal assets of those other owners in order to collect any past-due payroll taxes your business owes. The agency can also come after the personal assets of your business's chief financial officer and its board of directors.

If you filed a personal Chapter 7 bankruptcy because your business is a sole proprietorship, at the end of the bankruptcy, the judge will discharge most, but not all, of the debts that were not paid. Those debts that are not discharged may include:

- Any debts that were not listed on your schedules
- Certain federal and state government penalties and fines
- Any taxes that you did not pay during the three years prior to the start of your bankruptcy
- Debts that are the result of luxury goods or services valued at more than $1,150 that you purchased with a credit card within 60 days of the date that you filed for bankruptcy
- Debts related to assets that you acquired through fraud, embezzlement, misuse of funds, etc.
- Secured debts that you reaffirmed during bankruptcy. As soon as your bankruptcy is over, you must begin paying these debts according to the terms of the agreement you worked out with your secured creditors. Reaffirmations are discussed in Chapter 6.
- Government-guaranteed student loans
- Debts that are the result of your arrest for driving under the influence or driving while intoxicated

Completing Your Business's Bankruptcy

If your business has filed for Chapter 11, it cannot get out of bankruptcy until a majority of its creditors has approved its reorganization plan and the bankruptcy judge has confirmed the plan. Once that happens, your business will be responsible for paying its debts according to the terms of the approved plan. If your business does not live up to the plan, its creditors can file motions with the court alleging that your business is in *substantial noncompliance* with its reorganization plan and asking that the court put your business into a Chapter 7 bankruptcy. A hearing will follow, and the judge will decide whether your business must be shut down.

If your business has filed for Chapter 7, its bankruptcy will be over once the trustee has paid as many of its debts as possible. The trustee will file a final accounting of the bankruptcy with the court.

Using Chapter 11 Bankruptcy to Stay in Business

Chapter 4 explained in general terms how your business can use Chapter 11 bankruptcy to deal with its debts, so that it can continue to operate and become profitable. It also provided an overview of the process. This chapter offers more detailed information about the Chapter 11 bankruptcy process. Among other things, it reviews issues to discuss with your business's bankruptcy attorney before filing, explains the various steps in the Chapter 11 process, highlights the power of your business's creditors in Chapter 11, and discusses some of the key decisions you will have to make during that process.

Before Your Business Files

Many small businesses have difficulty completing a Chapter 11 bankruptcy, because the rules that govern the process are very complicated and give creditors a lot of power over its speed and direction. As a result, when faced with too little cash, little if any access to credit, and hostile creditors, many small businesses end up having to convert their Chapter 11 bankruptcy to a Chapter 7. However, the appropriate prebankruptcy planning, done with the help of an experienced bankruptcy attorney, can help increase the likelihood that your business will be able to complete its Chapter 11.

> # HOT TIP
>
> If you begin planning for your business's bankruptcy soon enough, and your business is incorporated, you may be able to dissolve it and deal with its debts by filing a Chapter 13 personal bankruptcy rather than a Chapter 11. A Chapter 13 bankruptcy is cheaper and easier-to-complete than a Chapter 11.

Here are the key issues you should address with the help of an experienced bankruptcy attorney during the pre–Chapter 11 planning process:

- *How will your business fund its operations during bankruptcy?* Coming up with enough cash to run your business will be a major challenge once it begins its Chapter 11 bankruptcy. Therefore, it is imperative that your business begin stockpiling as much cash as possible before it files. An adequate "war chest" is essential because:
  - Many vendors and suppliers will only work with your business on a cash basis after it has filed for bankruptcy.
  - After your business's bankruptcy begins, it will not be able to use its cash collateral without the court's permission. Cash collateral includes the receivables, rental income, bank accounts, securities, etc., that your business used to secure loans, lines of credit, and other sources of credit. When your business files a motion with the court asking for permission to use some of its cash collateral, the creditor with the lien on the collateral will probably file an objection to the motion with the bankruptcy court. After holding a hearing on the motion, the judge will decide whether or not your business can use the collateral, and under what conditions. Most likely, the judge will rule in favor of your business, but as a condition, he or she will probably order your business to make regular payments to the creditor.
  - Your business will need the court's permission to obtain additional secured credit. Again, after your business asks the court for permission to do this, some of its creditors may file

objections to the request. After holding hearings on the matter, the bankruptcy judge will decide whether or not your business can apply for the credit it needs to complete its Chapter 11 bankruptcy, and under what conditions.

WARNING

The more hearings that occur during the Chapter 11 process, the longer it will take your business to complete its bankruptcy, and the more the bankruptcy will cost your business. In fact, if there are too many hearings, the bankruptcy may become so expensive and time consuming that it will have to be converted to a Chapter 7.

- Your business will need the court's permission to generate operating capital by selling its assets—vehicles, office equipment, machinery, receivables, and so on. Again, if any of your business's creditors formally objects to the sale of an asset, the court will decide whether or not the sale can go forward after holding a hearing on the matter.
- Your business will need cash to pay for the services of a good bankruptcy attorney. In addition, during the bankruptcy process, the attorney may need to hire a CPA, a property appraiser, and other professionals. Your business will need money to pay them, too. Figure 5.1 reviews possible sources of operating capital for your business while it is in Chapter 11.

• *Which creditors will oppose your business's bankruptcy, and what is the best way to deal with them?* Creditors who are hostile to the bankruptcy may try to derail it or try to extract costly concessions from your business by filing various motions intended to interfere with your management decisions and increase your business's bankruptcy expenses. Because your business cannot get out of a Chapter 11 bankruptcy unless a majority of its creditors vote to approve its reorganization plan, the more time you have to develop strategies for dealing with hostile creditors, the more likely it is that your business's reorganiza-

FIGURE 5.1
Possible Sources of Operating Capital

If your business does not have enough cash to finance its operations during the Chapter 11 process, it will try to obtain the funds it needs by filing motions with the court. In the motions, you will ask the court for permission to use your business's cash collateral, to sell some of its assets, and/or to borrow money. In response, some of your business's creditors will almost certainly file objections to those motions with the court. Filing motions and dealing with creditor objections will cost your business additional money and slow down the progress of its bankruptcy. Obviously, therefore, the more cash your business can raise before its bankruptcy begins, the better. The following list highlights possible sources of prefiling cash:

- Sell assets that your business does not need.

- Raise prices, assuming an increase in prices will not discourage sales.

- Reduce staff.

- Contract with another company to use any excess capacity your business may have. For example, your business may be able to lease out unused office, retail, or manufacturing space.

- Borrow money, assuming your business has assets that it can use to secure a new loan. If your business's finances are in extremely bad shape, it may not be able to qualify for a new loan, and all of its assets may already be securing debt.

- Sell your business's receivables to a factor, assuming they are not already pledged as collateral. A *factor* is a business that buys receivables and then assumes the risk of collecting them.

tion efforts will succeed. In fact, if you begin planning soon enough, your business's bankruptcy attorney can begin building support for its reorganization early on in the process.

- *How will you manage the day-to-day details of running your business once its bankruptcy begins?* You will have a lot on your plate once your business is in Chapter 11. Among other things, you will have to:

- Prepare for and attend court hearings.
- Work with your business's attorney to resolve creditor problems.
- Help the attorney prepare a disclosure statement and reorganization plan for your business.
- Deal with secured creditors that want to take back assets essential to the continued operation of your business.
- Finance the ongoing operation of your business.
- Make whatever changes are necessary for your business to become profitable.
- Manage your employees, some of whom may be upset that your business is in bankruptcy.
- Comply with all of the bankruptcy court's reporting requirements.

In other words, the bankruptcy will take up your time, add stress to your life, and drain your energy. In essence, once your business's Chapter 11 has begun, you will have four jobs—run your business, work with its bankruptcy attorney, comply with any court orders, and meet the requirements of federal bankruptcy law. Therefore, you and your key management team should spend time thinking about how best to keep your business running smoothly during the bankruptcy process. To do that, you may need to make changes in personnel, procedures, and policies, among other things.

Other Steps to Take Before Filing

In addition to helping you address the bankruptcy-related issues outlined in the previous section, your business's bankruptcy attorney may also advise you to do the following before filing:

- Get your business's secured assets appraised and insured. Your business's attorney will have to provide the trustee with proof that these assets are adequately insured.
- File any past-due federal tax returns for your business. If your business is a sole proprietorship, the attorney will advise you to file all past-due personal tax returns.
- Make certain that the decision to file for bankruptcy is reflected in the minutes of your business's board meetings, if your business is incorporated.

When Your Business Is a Sole Proprietorship

The majority of the bankruptcy information and advice in this book relates to a small, closely held corporation that you may own with your spouse, siblings, a friend, and so on. However, this chapter and Chapter 6 provide bankruptcy-related information and advice specifically for the owners of sole proprietorships, because those owners face bankruptcy-related risks and decisions that corporate owners don't. The main reason for the difference is that if your business is a sole proprietorship and you want to deal with its problems through bankruptcy, you will have to file a *personal,* not a business, bankruptcy. In the eyes of the law, you and your business are one and the same. In other words, your business's debts and assets are your personal debts and assets. A corporation, on the other hand, has a legal and financial identity that is separate from its owner's. Therefore, its assets are its own and, in most cases, its debts are, too.

WARNING

Creditors that your sole proprietorship owes money to can go after your personal assets to collect any debts your business does not pay, because the law views you and your business as one and the same.

WARNING

If your corporation withholds taxes from the wages of its employees but does not pass on that money to the IRS as it is supposed to, the IRS can try to collect its tax money by going after your personal assets, because you are the business owner. In addition, your corporation's creditors can come after your personal assets if you personally guaranteed any of the money that your business owes to them.

You should also know that if your business is a sole proprietorship and you want to use bankruptcy to try to save it, you may be eligible to file a Chapter 13 reorganization bankruptcy rather than a Chapter 11. Whether you are eligible depends on the amount of debt that you owe. Figure 5.2 summarizes the benefits of Chapter 13 bankruptcy compared to Chapter 11, and explains when you can file for Chapter 13.

FIGURE 5.2
Filing for Bankruptcy When Your Business Is a Sole Proprietorship

When your business is a sole proprietorship and you want to save it by filing for bankruptcy, depending on how much personal and business-related debt you owe, you will either file a Chapter 11 reorganization or a Chapter 13 reorganization. A Chapter 13 bankruptcy is a personal, not a business, bankruptcy and therefore is not available to corporations or partnerships.

You are eligible to file for Chapter 13 if you owe less than $290,525 in unsecured debt and less than $871,550 in secured debt. These debt limits change periodically, so if your business is a sole proprietorship and you want to file Chapter 13, contact a bankruptcy attorney for information about the current limits.

Filing a Chapter 13 rather than a Chapter 11 is advantageous, because the Chapter 13 process is faster, less expensive, and easier to complete. For example, the court filing fee for a Chapter 13 bankruptcy is *just* $185, compared to $835 for a Chapter 11 bankruptcy. Also, attorney's fees and court costs are less with a Chapter 13. For detailed information on Chapter 13 bankruptcy, read my book, *The Bankruptcy Kit*, 2nd edition (Dearborn Trade Publishing, 1996).

A key difference between the two types of reorganization bankruptcies is that in a Chapter 13 you can exempt assets from the bankruptcy, up to a specific dollar amount. That means you may be able to pay less toward your debts. Therefore, be sure to take advantage of all the exemptions you are entitled to. Your bankruptcy attorney will help you do that. When you are deciding which exemptions to take, you may be able to choose between the exemptions in the federal Bankruptcy Code and your state's exemptions, which tend to be more generous than the federal ones. Florida and Texas offer especially generous exemptions, for example.

Filing the Right Paperwork

To begin your business's bankruptcy, your attorney will file a bankruptcy petition with the bankruptcy court in your district and pay a filing fee. At that point, an automatic stay will go into effect, which will put an immediate stop to most creditor collection actions. Although the court is responsible for notifying each of your business's creditors about the automatic stay, the notification will probably not happen immediately. Therefore, your business's attorney will contact them right away.

Early in the bankruptcy process, either at the same time that your business's bankruptcy petition is filed or within 15 days of the filing, your attorney will also file detailed schedules of your business's debts and assets with the court. He or she will prepare the schedules using information that you provide. That information will include tax returns for the past two years, mortgage agreements, leases, other contracts, and so on. The attorney will also prepare and file with the court a statement of your business's financial affairs.

Your business's debt schedules will list the names of your business's creditors, their addresses, the amount of money that your business owes to each of the creditors, and the date that your business acquired each debt. Your business's asset schedules will describe each of its assets together with a current, or market, value for each asset. An asset's market value represents the amount of money for which you could sell the asset today, not how much you paid for the asset.

WARNING

If your business's bankruptcy attorney does not file the appropriate paperwork by the applicable deadlines, the bankruptcy judge will probably dismiss your business's bankruptcy.

Your attorney will also file a disclosure statement and a reorganization plan within 120 days of the start of the bankruptcy. The information in the disclosure statement is intended to help your business's creditors and the bankruptcy judge decide whether to approve your business's reorganization plan. However, before your creditors can vote for or against the plan, the judge must approve your business's disclosure statement. If it is not approved, your business can amend the disclosure statement and try again to get it approved.

During those 120 days, your business has an exclusive right to file a reorganization plan for itself. If it misses that deadline, however, your business's creditors can file their own reorganization plans for your business, unless the bankruptcy attorney files a *motion to extend time for the exclusive right to file* and the motion is granted.

Debtor in Possession

Your business will assume a new identity as soon as its Chapter 11 bankruptcy begins. It will become a *debtor in possession,* which signifies that your business is in control of its own affairs and not in the hands of the bankruptcy trustee. Your business must open a new bank account as debtor in possession—the words will be printed on its checks—and it must use this account throughout the bankruptcy, rather than the account it is currently using.

Even though your business will be in charge of its own affairs during the Chapter 11 process, the trustee will be "watching over its shoulders." Among other things, the trustee will monitor your business to ensure that it complies with all of the rules of Chapter 11 and does not do anything that might harm the interests of its creditors. In addition, your business will have to provide the trustee with monthly operating reports, so that the trustee can keep track of its finances. If your business does not file these reports, if the trustee decides that your business's bankruptcy is not going well, or if the business is not acting in the best interests of its creditors, the trustee will file a motion with the court asking that the judge convert your business's bankruptcy to a Chapter 7, or to have the bankruptcy dismissed.

HOT TIP

It is a good idea to hire an accountant to help you comply with the Chapter 11 reporting requirements, because meeting these requirements can be quite time consuming.

FIGURE 5.3
Chronology of a Chapter 11 Bankruptcy

This chronology reflects the typical order of events in a Chapter 11 bankruptcy. However, the sequence of events can vary from bankruptcy to bankruptcy, so don't be surprised if your business's Chapter 11 progresses a little differently than the one outlined here.

1. You meet with your business's bankruptcy attorney to do the appropriate prebankruptcy planning.

2. The attorney initiates your business's bankruptcy by filing a petition with the federal bankruptcy court.

3. The *automatic stay* goes into effect.

4. The attorney files your business's schedules of debts and assets, statement of financial affairs, etc.

5. Your business files a motion with the bankruptcy court seeking permission to use its cash collateral.

6. Your business's creditors are notified that your business has filed for bankruptcy, and they begin filing *proof of claims* with the court.

7. Your business's attorney prepares and files an initial debtor's report with the bankruptcy trustee.

8. You, as business owner, your business's bankruptcy attorney, and the trustee meet at an initial debtor's conference. This meeting and the first creditors meeting may happen at the same time.

9. The creditors meeting takes place.

10. The bankruptcy attorney files your business's disclosure statement and reorganization plan with the court.

11. Your business's creditors file objections to your business's disclosure statement and to its reorganization plan. Hearings will be held to consider their objections.

12. The bankruptcy judge decides whether to accept your business's disclosure statement.

13. Your business's creditors vote to accept or reject its reorganization plan.

14. The judge confirms (approves) or denies the plan. If the plan is approved, your business's bankruptcy will be over. If the plan is not approved, your business can amend it and try to get the amended plan approved. Otherwise, your attorney will convert your business's bankruptcy to a Chapter 7 liquidation, and your business will shut down.

Your business must pay the trustee a quarterly fee while it is in bankruptcy. The amount of the fee will be based on a formula that takes into account your business's total revenues during the previous quarter as well as its total expenses. The quarterly fee will be no less than $250 and no more than $10,000.

As this chapter has already explained, while your business is in Chapter 11, you will need the court's permission to do some of the things that you used to do as a normal part of running the business. For example, you will need the court's okay to:

- Hire an attorney, CPA, appraiser, or some other professional to help your business.
- Use your business's cash collateral. The "Motions to Use Cash Collateral" section of this chapter discusses cash collateral.
- Take on more debt.

HOT TIP

If your business needs to borrow money while it is in bankruptcy, its best prospect for a loan may be a creditor to whom it already owes money. The lender may believe that lending your business additional money will increase its chances for getting the money it has already loaned your business.

WARNING

It is becoming increasingly difficult for *debtors in possession* to obtain new financing, because a growing number of lenders have decided that lending money to those businesses is simply not worth the risk. If your business does find a lender that will work with it, be prepared to pay a high rate of interest on the money—12 percent or higher.

- Purchase or sell an asset, unless the transaction is a normal part of your business's operations. For example, if you own a clothing store, you do not need the court's permission to buy and sell clothing. However, you *would* need its permission to sell the fixtures and computer equipment in the store, your business's truck, and so on. When the sale of an asset is outside the normal course of business, you must notify your business's creditors and the trustee of your intention to sell the asset at least 20 days prior to the sale by filing a motion with the court. There will be a hearing on the motion.

Ordinarily, in a Chapter 11 bankruptcy, your business will need the court's permission to assume, reject, or assign any unexpired, or executory, leases or contracts.

The Power of Chapter 11 Creditors

Your business's creditors can wield considerable power in its Chapter 11. In fact, they can make the difference between a successful reorganization and a failed one. Therefore, your business's attorney will spend much of his or her time, before and after the start of its bankruptcy, meeting with and negotiating with creditors.

There are several reasons why Chapter 11 creditors are so powerful. One key reason is that your business cannot get out of bankruptcy unless a majority of its creditors vote to approve its reorganization plan. Without their approval, your business will have to convert its bankruptcy to a Chapter 7 liquidation, unless the judge okays a *cramdown*. Cramdowns are discussed later in this chapter.

Another important reason for the power of creditors in a Chapter 11 is that throughout the bankruptcy process, they can try to protect their interests and/or derail your business's bankruptcy by filing different motions with the court. Each time they file a motion, a hearing will be scheduled, so that the bankruptcy judge can hear all sides of the issue. After the hearing, the judge will decide the motion, unless your business and the creditor that filed the motion resolve your differences outside of court. Meanwhile, each motion will delay the completion of your business's bankruptcy and will cost it more money, because preparing for hearings and filing *responses* to the motions will take up the time of your business's attorney. One of the most common motions in a Chapter 11 is a *motion to lift the automatic stay.* The motion is discussed later in this chapter.

> ## WARNING
>
> The more motions creditors file during your business's bankruptcy, the more expensive the bankruptcy will be and the longer it will take your business to complete the process. Also, the more motions, the more likely your business will miss the 120 days during which it has an exclusive right to file its reorganization plan and will have to convert to a Chapter 7 bankruptcy.

After Your Business's Chapter 11 Begins

Once your business's creditors have been notified that it is in bankruptcy, the court will establish a deadline, or *bar date,* by which they must file a proof of claim with the court. A *proof of claim* is a document that establishes a creditor's right to be paid by your business and indicates how much money the creditor thinks it is owed by your business.

If a creditor does not file a proof of claim by the bar date, your business can file a *motion to bar the claim* in an effort to eliminate that particular debt from its bankruptcy. The creditor can file a *response* to the motion. At a hearing on your business's motion, the judge will hear arguments from your business's attorney and the creditor's, if the creditor has filed a response. If the creditor does not file a response, the judge will probably grant your business's motion, which means that your business will not have to pay the debt.

At any point during its bankruptcy, your business can object to a creditor's proof of claim. For example, your business may object to:

- The amount of a claim
- The validity of a claim
- The value that a secured creditor has placed on its collateral
- How a creditor's claim has been classified.

Your business's attorney may file this objection in an effort to get the court to reclassify the claim as a lower-priority debt or even to get the claim eliminated from the bankruptcy.

If your business objects to a creditor's claim, the creditor will have 20 days to respond. If the creditor does not respond by the deadline, your business's motion will be granted. If the creditor does file a response within the 20-day time frame, a hearing will be scheduled, and after listening to arguments from both sides, the judge will rule on the matter. During the hearing, your business will have to provide credible evidence to support its motion, and if it cannot, the creditor that filed a response will have to prove why the claim that it filed is valid.

Motions to Lift the Automatic Stay

Throughout the bankruptcy process, your business's secured creditors may file *motions to lift the automatic stay* in order to get the court's permission to take back their collateral. Whenever a motion is filed, a hearing on the motion will be held within 30 days. Your business must file a response. If your business does not, the court will lift the automatic stay, so that the creditor who filed the motion can take back its collateral.

If your business does file a response, its attorney may contact the creditor's attorney prior to the hearing in an effort to negotiate a way for your business to keep the asset. If the negotiations don't work, the judge will decide the matter.

Most likely, the judge will let your business keep collateral that is essential to its reorganization, assuming your business can make monthly *adequate protection payments* to the creditor. The judge will decide the amount and the timing of the payments. For example, the judge may order your business to make regular monthly payments, according to the terms of its contract with the creditor, or to make interest-only payments for a set period of time.

Filing Motions to Use Cash Collateral

A *motion to use cash collateral* is another motion commonly filed by businesses that file for Chapter 11. This motion is important because without access to the cash resources your business needs to fund its operations during the bankruptcy, your business will not be able to complete the Chapter 11 process and will have to convert its bankruptcy to a Chapter 7. In fact, access to its cash collateral is so important to the outcome of your business's Chapter 11 bankruptcy that your bankruptcy attorney may begin filing motions to use cash collateral on an emergency basis as soon as your business's bankruptcy begins—maybe even at the same time that he or she files the bankruptcy petition.

Motions to use cash collateral tend to be among the most hotly contested types of motions in a Chapter 11. Therefore, if your business files one of these motions, be prepared for the creditor with the lien on the cash collateral that your business is asking permission to use to file a *response* with the court. In anticipation of the creditor's response, your business's bankruptcy attorney may contact some of its secured creditors immediately following the start of the bankruptcy to negotiate agreements with them that will let your business have access to its cash collateral. These negotiations can help your business avoid potentially long and costly cash collateral battles after its bankruptcy has begun.

The judge will probably give your business access to its cash collateral if he or she believes that the collateral is critical to your business's reorganization efforts. However, to help protect the interests of creditors with liens on the collateral, the judge may limit your business's use of it and may require that your business insure the collateral, pay interest on the collateral, give the creditors additional collateral, or make monthly payments to the creditors, etc.

The Creditors Meeting

Your business's creditors meeting will take place 20 to 40 days after the automatic stay has gone into effect. The U.S. Trustee will set a date for the meeting and will notify the creditors about the meeting, which will take place at the federal bankruptcy courthouse in your district or at some other location the U.S. Trustee selects. The U.S. Trustee will run the creditors meeting.

Your business's attorney will attend the meeting, but you must be there, too. In fact, if you do not attend, your business's bankruptcy may be dismissed, and you may have no other option than to liquidate the business through Chapter 7.

The creditors meeting is open to any of your business's creditors, secured or unsecured. However, as you learned in Chapter 4, secured creditors are most inclined to attend, because they usually have more at stake in the bankruptcy than your business's unsecured creditors.

The creditors meeting serves a number of purposes. First, it gives the U.S. Trustee and your business's creditors an opportunity to ask you questions, which you will have to answer under oath. For example, the U.S. Trustee will ask questions to make sure that:

- Your asset and debt schedules are complete and accurate.
- All of the assets in your business's bankruptcy estate are adequately insured.
- You understand that your business has an obligation to file monthly operating reports with the court and pay the court a fee each quarter.

HOT TIP

Prior to the creditors meeting, your business's bankruptcy attorney will prepare you to answer the trustee's questions as well as questions from your business's creditors.

If you don't know how to answer any of the questions you are asked at the meeting, just say so. You will not be penalized. Don't make up an answer. Also, if you realize that information was left off of one of your business's schedules, or that there is some other problem with the schedules, let the trustee know. You will not get in trouble.

WARNING

Your business's bankruptcy may be dismissed, and you may be criminally prosecuted, if you lie at the creditors meeting or if the court determines that you knowingly tried to conceal assets from the court.

At the meeting, your business's creditors will probably ask questions about the financial condition of your business and about your plans for making it profitable. Your secured creditors may also want to know what steps you have taken to protect their collateral, and whether the collateral is in good condition and adequately insured. They will also be interested in finding out whether your business owes taxes on the collateral, and what your business intends to do with the collateral, among other things.

Be prepared to have some of your business's creditors express anger and hostility toward you and your business at the creditors meeting. However, as difficult as it may be to keep your cool, don't respond in kind. If you lash out at the creditors or act defensive, you may alienate them even more than they are already, and you may also anger creditors that were neutral toward your business up until then. Remember, your business needs all the creditor support it can get, because to get out of a Chapter 11 bankruptcy, a majority of your creditors must support the reorganization plan.

In addition to answering creditors' questions, the creditors meeting also provides you with a venue for lobbying on behalf of your business and its reorganization efforts. In essence, the meeting represents an opportunity to sell creditors on the idea that a reorganization makes sense for your business and for them—and that it is possible, with their cooperation. Not only will creditors' support help minimize the number of motions they may file during your business's bankruptcy, but it will also increase the likelihood that they will approve your business's reorganization plan.

The creditors meeting also gives your business's bankruptcy attorney an opportunity to begin negotiating the details of its reorganization plan with its creditors—if those negotiations have not already begun. Getting as many issues as possible ironed out at the creditors meeting will help shorten the duration of your business's bankruptcy and minimize the cost.

Don't Miss These Deadlines!

During the 120 days following the start of your business's bankruptcy, it will have an exclusive right to prepare and file its own reorganization plan with the court, and it will have an additional 80 days to get the plan approved by its creditors. If your business misses either deadline, its creditors can prepare and file their own reorganization plans for your business. If they file multiple plans, the judge will decide which plan is in the best interest of your business's creditors, and that will be the plan that your creditors vote on.

> ## WARNING
>
> Most creditor-developed reorganization plans lead to the liquidation of a business.

> ## HOT TIP
>
> If it becomes obvious that your business can't meet the 120-day plan filing deadline, your attorney can ask the court to extend the deadline.

The "All about Reorganization Plans" section of this chapter tells you more about reorganization plans. First, however, the next section discusses disclosure statements, because your business's creditors can't vote on its reorganization plan until the bankruptcy judge has approved its disclosure statement.

The Disclosure Statement

During the 120 days following the start of your business's bankruptcy, your business must also prepare a *disclosure statement.* Ordinarily, your business will file its disclosure statement and reorganization plan with the court at the same time.

The purpose of the disclosure statement is to provide your business's creditors, as well as the U.S. Trustee and the bankruptcy judge, with "adequate information" to help them decide whether or not to approve your business's reorganization plan. Although federal bankruptcy law does not define adequate information, your business's disclosure statement will probably address the following:

- The current state of your business's finances, including a summary of its assets and debts

- A projection of your business's future revenues and expenses. Creditors that will be paid out of future earnings will be particularly interested in this information.
- A brief history of your business, including an explanation of why and how its current financial problems developed
- A short discussion of any litigation that may be pending against your business, as well as any pending litigation that your business has initiated. This discussion should state clearly how you anticipate each lawsuit will affect your business's reorganization.
- A list of all the owners of your business, as well as a summary of the qualifications and experience of your business's management team
- An explanation of why your business filed for Chapter 11 bankruptcy, its objectives in filing, how your business intends to achieve those objectives, as well as an overview of how your business's bankruptcy has gone so far
- A summary of your business's reorganization plan and an argument for why it should be approved

---

HOT TIP

Base your business's disclosure statement on facts, not on your opinions and hopes. If you include your opinions in the statement, back them up with facts whenever you can.

Your business's creditors can file objections to its disclosure statement after the statement has been filed with the court. The creditors may object, because, among other reasons, they believe that the statement is inaccurate or they do not think it provides them with enough information to be able to make a decision about your business's reorganization plan.

The court will hold hearings on the creditors' objections. After the hearings, your business's attorney may decide to amend the disclosure statement to reflect the concerns of your business's creditors.

Once the bankruptcy judge has approved your business's disclosure statement, your business can proceed to the next step in the Chapter 11 bankruptcy process—getting its reorganization plan approved.

All about Reorganization Plans

Most likely, almost as soon as he or she is hired, your business's attorney will begin to prepare a reorganization plan for your business. In fact, if your business hires its attorney soon enough, he or she may begin working on the plan even before filing your business's bankruptcy petition. Given the relatively short amount of time your business has to prepare and file its reorganization plan after its bankruptcy begins, coupled with the amount of work that usually goes into a plan, most attorneys need all the time they can get. Once your attorney has completed the plan, he or she will file the plan and the disclosure statement with the court.

Once the reorganization plan has been filed, some of your business's creditors may indicate that they are unhappy with certain aspects of it and, as a result, you and the attorney may decide to amend it. For example, the creditors may be displeased with the amount of money your business wants to put into the plan, how much your business proposes to pay them, the timing of the payments, and/or the conditions that may apply to the payments. To reduce the number of problems that your business's creditors raise, the attorney will probably try to involve them in the plan development process sooner rather than later. Early involvement will provide the attorney with an opportunity to turn doubters of your reorganization efforts into supporters, and will increase the likelihood that your business's creditors will approve the final reorganization plan after it is put to a vote.

Your business's attorney will have considerable freedom regarding what to put in the reorganization plan. However, federal bankruptcy law does require that the plan include specific kinds of information and do particular things. For example, the plan must:

- Classify each of the valid claims filed by your business's creditors. How the plan groups creditor claims is strategically important, because your business's creditors will vote for or against its plan on a class-by-class or group-by-group basis, and because certain groupings will make approval more likely. The attorney can classify the claims in a way that benefits your business, so long as he or she has a good rationale for the groupings. For example, the attorney may group together all claims under $1,000 or all unsecured claims. However, federal bankruptcy law says that your business's reorganization plan must:

- Treat all claims within the same class in a similar or equivalent manner, unless a creditor agrees to treatment that is less favorable than the rest of the creditors in its same class.

- Provide for the payment of your business's debts according to the priority of claims established in federal bankruptcy law. If your business does not have enough money to pay everything that it owes, it must pay its most important debts—the highest-priority debts—first. Its less important debts will probably be paid on a proportional basis, which means that lower-priority creditors will not receive the full amount of money that your business owes to them.

- Group together all administrative claims and priority tax claims.

• Indicate which claims or classes of claims are unimpaired. An *unimpaired claim* is a debt that your business has never defaulted on. Examples of priority claims include wage claims filed by your business's employees, up to $4,650 per employee; wage benefit claims filed by your employees, up to a set amount per employee; and unsecured tax claims. By the way, your business can have up to six years to pay the balance on its past-due federal tax debt, including interest.

H O T   T I P

Whenever possible, avoid a reorganization plan that obligates your business to make lump sum payments to its creditors. Those payments are apt to put a big financial strain on your business and may even cripple it.

• Explain how your business proposes to deal with each valid *impaired claim,* including how much your business intends to pay each impaired creditor, if anything, and the timing of any payments. Most of the claims in your business's bankruptcy will be impaired. An *impaired claim* is a debt that your business does not intend to pay according to the terms of its original contract with the creditor that it owes the money to. For example, if your business's reorganization plan shows that your business will pay everything that it owes to a particular creditor, but that your business intends to take longer to pay the money than what is stipulated in its original contract with the creditor, then that creditor's claim is impaired. Creditors that will receive nothing at all in your business's bankruptcy also have impaired claims. However, federal bankruptcy law requires that your business's impaired creditors receive at least the present value of what they would have received if your business had filed for Chapter 7 instead of Chapter 11.

- Explain how your business intends to deal with each of its secured debts. In bankruptcy, a secured creditor can be fully secured or undersecured. A *fully secured creditor* is one whose collateral is worth the same amount or more than the balance on the debt that the collateral secures. A fully secured creditor is entitled to receive the full amount of its claim in your business's reorganization. An *undersecured creditor* is one whose collateral is worth less than the balance on the debt that the collateral secures. In bankruptcy, an undersecured creditor is treated as though it has two claims—a secured claim and an unsecured claim. The creditor is entitled to payment on its secured claim up to the value of its interest in the collateral. The balance of its claim is an unsecured debt.

- Explain how your business plans to implement its reorganization. Your business may have to sell assets, modify liens, cut staff, cure defaults, transfer property, and so on, in order to take care of its debts and become profitable.

Putting It to a Vote

Once the bankruptcy attorney has prepared a disclosure statement and reorganization plan for your business, he or she will send a copy of the disclosure statement to the bankruptcy judge and to your business's creditors. The creditors can file objections to the statement, if they believe it is missing information that will help them decide whether to approve the reorganization plan. There will be a hearing on the disclosure statement, and if no objections are filed, the judge will approve the statement and set a date for a hearing on the reorganization plan. This hearing is called a *confirmation hearing.* If creditors do file objections to your business's disclosure statement, the judge will rule on them after listening to all sides at the hearing. As a result, the attorney may amend the disclosure statement so that the judge will approve it.

Once your business's disclosure statement has been approved, the attorney will mail certain information to each of your creditors together with a cover letter. The materials will include:

- A copy of your business's reorganization plan
- A copy of the disclosure statement that was approved by the judge
- An official ballot that the creditors can use to vote for or against your business's plan
- Information regarding the deadline by which creditors must return their ballots to the court
- The date of the confirmation hearing
- Any other information the court directs your business to mail to its creditors

The attorney will also send the U.S. Trustee copies of the reorganization plan and disclosure statement.

After they receive your business's reorganization plan, your creditors will have 45 to 60 days to vote for or against the plan and file objections to it. Ideally, your business's attorney will have already resolved all possible objections to the plan before it was filed, but there will probably be at least a few objections.

Meanwhile, the attorney will contact your business's creditors in order to urge them to fill out and return their ballots to the court. He or she will also keep a running tally of how the votes are going, so that you will know whether there will be enough votes to approve it. For the plan to be approved, at least 51 percent of your business's creditors in each impaired class and at least two-thirds of the total value of all the claims in a class must vote for the plan.

If your business's attorney determines that your creditors are going to reject the plan, he or she can withdraw it and go back to the drawing board. If that happens, the balloting process will have to begin all over again. Another option is for your business's attorney to ask the court for a *cramdown*. If your business cannot afford to remain in Chapter 11 and keep trying for approval, and if a cramdown is not an option, your business's bankruptcy will have to be converted to a Chapter 7. Cramdowns are discussed in greater detail in the next section of this chapter.

At the confirmation hearing, your business's attorney will present the judge with a tally of the creditors' votes, and the judge will hear any objections to the plan. If there are enough votes for the plan's approval, the judge will probably confirm it. First, however, the judge will consider the following:

- Is the plan fair to your business's creditors?
- Is the plan *adequate;* that is, does it pay enough to your business's creditors?
- Does the plan provide for the full payment of all priority claims?
- Did your business propose the plan in good faith; that is, is no fraud involved?
- Does the plan comply with all applicable provisions of the federal bankruptcy law?
- Has each claim holder within a particular class either accepted the plan or will each claim holder receive at least the liquidation value of its claim through the plan?

A Cramdown—Your Business's Last Hope for a Successful Reorganization

Don't give up hope if your business cannot get enough of its creditors to vote for its reorganization plan. The bankruptcy judge may agree to confirm the plan anyway through a *cramdown.* The judge will decide the cramdown at the time of confirmation.

Your business is eligible to attempt a cramdown if its reorganization plan was not approved and if the plan meets all of the requirements of federal bankruptcy law. For example, at least one of your business's impaired creditors must have voted for the plan, the plan cannot discriminate against any class of claims that voted against it, and the plan must be fair to all of the creditors in those classes.

Different rules apply to cramdowns, depending on whether your business is attempting a cramdown against its secured or unsecured creditors. For example, to get a cramdown against a class of secured creditors, your business's reorganization plan must allow the creditors in that class to retain their liens and provide for cash payments to those creditors equal to the value of their collateral. As an alternative, the court may allow your business to transfer the liens to other assets your business may own, assuming that the present value of the other assets is equivalent to the current value of the creditors' collateral.

For your business's reorganization plan to be confirmed against the wishes of a class of unsecured creditors, your business must give them at least as much as they would have received if your business had filed for Chapter 7.

Once the Plan Is Approved

Once your business's plan is confirmed, the court will issue an *order of confirmation.* At that point, the automatic stay will end and your business will be out of bankruptcy and will not be a debtor in possession anymore. Your business and its creditors will be responsible for living up to the terms of the approved plan.

If your business is incorporated, the order of confirmation will discharge any preconfirmation debts that will not be paid according to the approved reorganization plan. Even if your business subsequently fails to live up to the terms of the plan, it will not have to pay those debts.

If you filed a personal bankruptcy because your business is a sole proprietorship, all of the preconfirmation debts that you did not agree to pay in your reorganization plan will be discharged, except for any unpaid debts that cannot be erased according to federal bankruptcy law.

If your business has trouble meeting any of the provisions in its reorganization plan once it is out of bankruptcy, your bankruptcy attorney can ask the court for permission to modify the plan, assuming there is good reason for the request. If the court denies the request, your business may have to file for Chapter 7 bankruptcy.

Also, your business's secured creditors can take back their collateral if your business does not live up to its plan obligations. Either way, your business will probably be forced into Chapter 7. The Chapter 7 bankruptcy process is explained in Chapter 6.

6

Ending Your Business through a Chapter 7 Liquidation Bankruptcy

A Chapter 7 liquidation bankruptcy may be the answer to your prayers, if your business is drowning in debt and there is little or no chance you can save it through a turnaround or a reorganization bankruptcy. Filing for Chapter 7 may be necessary because:

- Your business owes too much debt relative to its income.
- Your business's creditors are extremely hostile to a reorganization.
- Your business does not have the money it needs to get through a reorganization.
- Your business's chances of becoming profitable through a turnaround or a reorganization bankruptcy are slim to none.
- You do not want to be in business anymore.
- You tried without success to save your business through a turnaround or a Chapter 11 bankruptcy.

This chapter takes you through the Chapter 7 process. It describes the role of the trustee and your business's creditors in a Chapter 7 bankruptcy, explains what will happen to the debts your business owes, and highlights the special issues you face if you run your business as a sole proprietorship.

Beginning Your Business's Chapter 7 Bankruptcy

To initiate your business's Chapter 7 bankruptcy, your bankruptcy attorney will file a bankruptcy petition in the bankruptcy court for the area where your business is located. The attorney will also pay the court a $200 filing fee.

The attorney will file other bankruptcy forms as well, including:

- *Schedules of your business's debts.* The attorney will prepare these schedules using information and records that you provide, including recent financial statements and tax returns for your business, current leases, and other contracts. Any debts not listed on the schedules will not be a part of your business's bankruptcy.

HOT TIP

It's a good idea to review your business's accounts payable records for the past several years to help ensure that the bankruptcy attorney has complete and accurate information about your business's outstanding debts. When you review those records, you may find debts that you have forgotten about, because creditors that your business owes money to stopped contacting you about the debts. Even so, your business still owes these creditors.

- *Schedules of your business's assets.* The attorney will describe the assets your business owns and will provide a current market value for each. *Market value* represents the amount of money that an asset is worth now, not the amount that you paid for it.
- *A statement of affairs.* This is a series of questions that you must answer as the owner of your business. Your answers will help the trustee and your business's creditors make certain that your business's schedules of assets and debts are complete and accurate, and that your business has not tried to conceal any assets from bankruptcy.

> ## WARNING
>
> If the trustee determines that your business attempted to hide assets, he or she will try to get those assets back, so that they can be sold and the sale proceeds used to pay off your business's debts. In addition, you may be criminally prosecuted.

As soon as your business's bankruptcy petition has been filed, the *automatic stay* will go into effect, which will halt most creditor collection actions against your business. The bankruptcy attorney will contact your business's creditors immediately to tell them about the automatic stay. Some time after that, the court will also notify the creditors about the automatic stay.

Your business will not continue to operate after its bankruptcy petition has been filed, and a private trustee appointed by the court will take control of it. Most private trustees are attorneys or CPAs.

The trustee will collect all of your business's assets and place a value on each one. To value them, the trustee may have to use professional appraisers, and the cost of their services will be included in your business's bankruptcy. Subsequently, the trustee will arrange to sell the unencumbered assets—the assets without liens—either through an auction or private sale. He or she will use the sale proceeds to pay as much as possible on your business's debts. The debts will be paid in the order of their priority according to federal bankruptcy law. See Chapter 4 for a discussion of the priority of debts in bankruptcy.

From start to finish, most small business Chapter 7 bankruptcies take about six months. However, if your business's bankruptcy is especially complex or it owes money to a lot of creditors, the bankruptcy could take longer to complete. Figure 6.1 provides an overview of the key events in a Chapter 7 bankruptcy.

The Trustee in a Chapter 7 Bankruptcy

The trustee in your business's Chapter 7 bankruptcy will not be a federal government employee like trustees in Chapter 11 bankruptcies. Instead, the trustee will be a private individual, probably a CPA or an

FIGURE 6.1
Sequence of Events in a Chapter 7 Bankruptcy

This figure provides a general overview of what you can expect as your business moves through the Chapter 7 bankruptcy process:

1. Your business files a bankruptcy petition with the court together with schedules of its assets and debts and a *statement of affairs.*

2. The automatic stay goes into effect, and your business's creditors are notified of the bankruptcy.

3. The bankruptcy court appoints a trustee to supervise the bankruptcy.

4. A creditors meeting takes place.

5. Your business's creditors file *proof of claim forms* with the bankruptcy court, if there is money to distribute.

6. The bankruptcy trustee takes title to your business's assets, places a value on each asset, and determines which ones can be sold.

7. The trustee oversees the sale of the assets and distributes the sale proceeds to your business's creditors according to the priority of their claims.

8. Once all of the money has been distributed, the trustee completes the final bankruptcy paperwork, and your business's bankruptcy is complete.

attorney. Also, the trustee will have considerably more responsibilities than a Chapter 11 trustee. For example, the trustee will take control of your business's assets as soon as its bankruptcy begins, and the assets will no longer belong to your business.

If you file a personal bankruptcy because your business is a sole proprietorship, the trustee will take control of all your nonexempt assets. Those assets may include the ones you use in your business as well as other nonbusiness assets. It will depend on which assets you have decided to exempt. The trustee will not control any of your exempt assets, which means that these assets will not be included in your bankruptcy and that you will be able to keep them. See Chapter 4 for an explanation of how bankruptcy exemptions work.

The trustee will also be responsible for:

- Ensuring that your business's schedules are complete and accurate.
- Confirming that your business did not make any illegal transfers or payments prior to filing for bankruptcy.
- Valuing each of your business's assets.
- Determining which assets can be liquidated and the best way to sell each of them.
- Presiding over your business's creditors meeting.
- Determining the validity of each of the *proof of claim forms* that your business's creditors file. The trustee will throw out any invalid proof of claims.
- Hiring appraisers, accountants, and any other professionals as necessary to help the trustee carry out his or her responsibilities in the bankruptcy. The trustee must get the court's permission to use the services of these and any other outside professionals.
- Informing your business's creditors about any hearings they are entitled to attend and any court decisions that affect them.
- Using the proceeds from the sale of your business's assets to pay the valid claims of your business's creditors according to their priority as established by federal bankruptcy law.
- Providing the court with a final report on the disposition of your business's assets.

The trustee will charge a fee for his or her services, which will come out of the funds generated by the sale of your business's assets. The amount of the fee will be based on the value of the assets that the trustee liquidates and distributes to your business's unsecured creditors.

The Creditors Meeting

Thirty to 40 days after your business's bankruptcy has begun, you will have to attend a creditor's meeting. Your business's bankruptcy attorney will accompany you to the meeting. During the meeting, the trustee will ask you questions, which you will have to answer under oath. Your business's creditors may ask you questions, too. Your business's secured creditors are more apt to attend the meeting than its unsecured creditors.

Before the date of the creditors meeting, your business's attorney will meet with you to review the questions you are likely to be asked

> ### HOT TIP
>
> Generally, Chapter 7 creditors tend to be less aggressive and hostile than creditors in a Chapter 11 bankruptcy.

> ### WARNING
>
> If you do not attend your business's creditors meeting, your bankruptcy will probably be dismissed and your business will lose all of the protections of bankruptcy. Therefore, if you cannot attend the meeting on the date for which it has been scheduled, let your attorney know so he or she can ask the court for an alternative date.

at the meeting. However, if you are asked a question that you do not know how to answer during the creditors meeting, just be honest and say so. You will not get in trouble. Don't make up an answer, because if you do and the bankruptcy judge finds out you lied, your business's bankruptcy will probably be dismissed and its assets will become fair game for its creditors. If you personally guaranteed any of those debts, and your business's creditors are unable to collect from your business, they will look to you for the money they are owed.

Here are some of the things that the trustee will probably ask you during the creditors meeting:

- Are your business's schedules of assets and debts accurate and complete? If you realize that an asset or debt has been left off a schedule, let the trustee know. You will not get in trouble.
- What method did you use to value your business's assets? If the trustee questions a particular value, he or she may ask the court's permission to get the asset appraised professionally.

W A R N I N G

If your business is a sole proprietorship and its bankruptcy is dismissed, your business's creditors can try to collect their debts by going after your personal assets.

- Did your business make any preferential payments to its creditors during the 90 days prior to the start of its bankruptcy? If it did, the trustee will cancel the payments and try to get back the money, so that the money can be distributed to your business's creditors according to the priority of their claims under federal bankruptcy law.
- Did you try to conceal any of your business's assets from the bankruptcy court by transferring them to another company or individual just prior to filing the bankruptcy petition? If the trustee determines that you did, he or she will void the transfers, and the assets will have to be returned to the trustee so that they can be sold.

W A R N I N G

If the trustee determines that you deliberately left an asset or debt off your business's schedules, you could be charged with a bankruptcy crime, which is a criminal offense.

- Did you borrow any money from your business within 90 days of the date that it filed for bankruptcy? If you did, the money will be treated as a preferential payment, and you will have to return the money to the trustee.
- Does your business have an income tax refund coming to it? The amount of the refund should be listed on your business's asset schedules.

- Is your business entitled to any money as a result of a lawsuit it is a party to? The lawsuit should also be listed on your business's asset schedules.

HOT TIP

If you file a personal Chapter 7 bankruptcy because your business is a sole proprietorship, you may be able to exempt a pending tax refund, financial judgment, or even an inheritance that you expect to receive or that you received within six months of filing your bankruptcy petition.

Creditor Claims and Objections

After the creditors meeting, your business's creditors will begin filing *proof of claims* with the bankruptcy court if there is money to disperse. Only those creditors that file valid claims by the bar date—the filing deadline set by the court—will be in line to have their claims paid. The judge will *bar the debts*—acknowledge that your business owes the debts but relieve your business from having to pay them—related to any creditors that miss the deadline.

The trustee may object to any claims that he or she believes are inaccurate or invalid. Also, your business's attorney may object to some of the claims. He or she may file an objection if you disagree with the amount of the claim or with the way that claim is classified, or if you do not believe that your business owes the debt, among other reasons. A hearing will be scheduled for each objection, and at the end of each hearing, the judge will rule how to handle the claim.

During the 60 days following the creditors meeting, your business's creditors may also file motions with the court. For example, some of your business's secured creditors, especially creditors who are owed a substantial amount of money by your business, may file *motions to lift the automatic stay* in order to get the court's permission to take back their collateral. However, the court will not give them that permission unless the creditors can prove that your business has no equity in the assets in question.

When Your Business Is a Sole Proprietorship

As you learned in Chapter 4, if your business is a sole proprietorship and you file Chapter 7 because your business has too much debt, you will file a personal, not a business, bankruptcy. This is because there is no distinction between you and your business in the eyes of the law. In other words, the law considers your business's debts and assets and your personal debts and assets to be one and the same.

If you run your business as a sole proprietorship, you will have to make some decisions in a Chapter 7 bankruptcy that you would not make if your business were a corporation. Among other things, you will have to decide:

- Which assets you want to exempt from the bankruptcy. See Chapter 4 for an explanation of how exemptions work. Depending on the state where your business is located, you may be able to choose between the federal exemptions and your state's exemptions. The trustee will take control of the assets that you do not exempt.
- Whether you want to redeem collateral or reaffirm a debt that is associated with a secured asset that you have exempted.

Figure 6.2 explains how reaffirmations and redemptions work.

W A R N I N G

You will have to pay your bankruptcy attorney a fee to handle a *redemption* or *reaffirmation*. That fee will be in addition to what you pay him or her to handle your bankruptcy.

Once you reaffirm a debt, and the court has approved your reaffirmation agreement, you will have 60 days to change your mind and cancel the agreement. If you do, you are required to send the creditor a written notice of your change of heart.

If you can't keep up with your payments on the debt that you reaffirmed after your bankruptcy is complete, the secured creditor that you owe the money to can take back its collateral and sell it. If the asset sells for less than the outstanding balance on your loan, you must pay the difference, or *deficiency*.

FIGURE 6.2
How Reaffirmations and Redemptions Work

When you file a personal bankruptcy, and you have exempted some of your secured assets from the bankruptcy, you may be able to use the redemption and reaffirmation processes to keep those assets. You must use these processes, because bankruptcy law does not allow you to just keep those secured assets without paying for them, even if they are exempt.

If the secured asset that you want to keep is worth *less* than what you owe on it, you can *redeem* the asset by paying the asset's value, in cash, to the creditor with a lien on that asset. For example, if you owe $1,000 on computer equipment, but the market value of the equipment is only $500, you can keep it by paying $500 to the creditor that has a lien on the equipment. First, however, you and the creditor will have to agree on what the equipment is worth now, and if you can't, the judge will decide after holding a court hearing on the matter.

If the secured asset that you want to keep is worth *more* than what you owe on it, you may be able hold on to the asset by *reaffirming* the debt that is associated with it. When you reaffirm a debt, you agree to pay the creditor according to the original contract, or you and the creditor agree to some other payment arrangement. Unlike a redemption, which requires that you make a lump sum payment to the secured creditor, you will make a series of payments to the creditor after your bankruptcy is over. You must also pay the creditor all the interest that has accrued on the debt. And, the creditor may make getting immediately caught up on your past-due loan balance a condition for agreeing with your request to reaffirm.

Completing the Chapter 7 Bankruptcy

After the trustee has finished paying as much as possible to as many of your business's creditors as possible, your business's bankruptcy case will be closed, your bankruptcy will be complete, and the automatic stay will be lifted. Once that happens, your business's creditors can come after your personal assets for any unpaid debts that you personally guaranteed as well as for any outstanding payroll taxes. In fact, you may have to file for Chapter 13 to protect your personal assets while you try to figure out a way to deal with those unpaid debts.

If you filed a personal bankruptcy because your business is a sole proprietorship, the court will formally discharge, or eliminate, most but not necessarily all of the debts the trustee did not pay or you did not reaffirm. Debts that do not get discharged include payroll taxes, past-due child support and alimony, unpaid government-guaranteed student loans, and fines and penalties due to a government entity. You will either receive a formal discharge order at a discharge hearing, or the court will mail the discharge papers to you.

Sample Chapter 11 Bankruptcy Forms

These forms may be purchased from BlumbergExcelsior, Inc., or any of its dealers. Reproduction prohibited.

Official Form B1, P1, 9-97   BlumbergExcelsior, Inc NYC 10013

United States Bankruptcy Court **District of**	**Voluntary Petition**

Name of Debtor (If individual, enter Last, First, Middle):	Name of Joint Debtor (Spouse) (Last, First, Middle):
All Other Names used by the debtor in the last 6 years (include married, maiden and trade names):	All Other Names used by the joint debtor in the last 6 years (include married, maiden and trade names):
Soc. Sec./Tax I.D. No. (If more than one, state all):	Soc. Sec./Tax I.D. No. (If more than one, state all):
Street Address of Debtor (No. and street, city, state, zip):	Street Address of Joint Debtor (No. and street, city, state, zip):
County of Residence or Principal Place of Business:	County of Residence or Principal Place of Business:
Mailing Address of Debtor (If different from street address):	Mailing Address of Joint Debtor (If different from street address):

Location of Principal Assets of Business Debtor
(If different from addresses listed above)

Information Regarding Debtor (Check the Applicable Boxes)

Venue (Check any applicable box)
☐ Debtor has been domiciled or has had a residence, principal place of business or principal assets in this District for 180 days immediately preceding the date of this petition or for a longer part of such 180 days than in any other District.
☐ There is a bankruptcy case concerning debtor's affiliate, general partner or partnership pending in this district

Type of Debtor (Check all boxes that apply)		**Chapter or Section of Bankruptcy Code Under Which the Pertition is Filed** (Check one box)
☐ Individual	☐ Railroad	☐ Chapter 7 ☐ Chapter 11 ☐ Chapter 13
☐ Corporation	☐ Stockbroker	☐ Chapter 9 ☐ Chapter 12
☐ Partnership	☐ Commodity Broker	☐ § 304-Case ancillary to foreign proceeding.
☐ Other		

Nature of Debt (Check one box) ☐ Consumer/Non-Business ☐ Business	**Filing Fee** (Check one box) ☐ Full Filing Fee attached.
Chapter 11 Small Business (Check all boxes that apply) ☐ Debtor is a small business as defined in 11 U.S.C. § 101. ☐ Debtor is and elects to be considered a small business under 11 U.S.C. § 1121(e) (Optional)	☐ Filing Fee to be paid in installments (Applicable to individuals only) Must attach signed application for the court's consideration certifying that the debtor is unable to pay fee except in installments. Rule 1006(b). See Official Form No. 3

Statistical/Administrative Information (Estimates Only)
☐ Debtor estimates that funds will be available for distribution to unsecured creditors.
☐ Debtor estimates that, after any exempt property is excluded and administrative expenses paid, there will be no funds available for distribution to unsecured creditors.

THIS SPACE FOR COURT USE ONLY

Estimated Number of Creditors	1-15	16-49	50-99	100-199	200-999	1000-over
	☐	☐	☐	☐	☐	☐

Estimated Assets						
$0 to $50,000	$50,001 to $100,000	$100,001 to $500,000	$500,001 to $1 million	$1,000,001 to $10 million	$10,000.001 to $100 million	More than $100 million
☐	☐	☐	☐	☐	☐	☐

Estimated Debts						
$0 to $50,000	$50,001 to $100,000	$100,001 to $500,000	$500,001 to $1 million	$1,000,001 to $10 million	$10,000.001 to $100 million	More than $100 million
☐	☐	☐	☐	☐	☐	☐

Official Form B1, P2, 9-01   ●   **Blumberg**Excelsior, Inc NYC 10013   ●

Voluntary Petition *(This page must be completed and filed in every case)*	Name of Debtor(s):

Prior Bankruptcy Case Filed Within Last 6 Years (If more than one, attach additional sheet)		
Location Where Filed:	Case Number:	Date Filed:

Pending Bankruptcy Case Filed by any Spouse, Partner, or Affiliate of this Debtor (If more than one, attach additional sheet.)		
Name of Debtor:	Case Number:	Date Filed:
District:	Relationship:	Judge:

Signatures

Signature(s) of Debtor(s) (Individual/Joint)

I declare under penalty of perjury that the information provided in this petition is true and correct.

[If petitioner is an individual whose debts are primarily consumer debts and has chosen to file under chapter 7] I am aware that I may proceed under chapter 7, 11,12,13 of title 11, United States Code, understand the relief available under each such chapter, and choose to proceed under chapter 7.

I request relief in accordance with the chapter of title 11, United States Code, specified in this petition.

X_____
Signature of Debtor

X_____
Signature of Joint Debtor

_____
Telephone (If not represented by attorney)

_____
Date

Signature of Attorney

X_____
Signature of Attorney for Debtor(s)

_____
Printed Name of Attorney for Debtor(s)

_____
Firm Name

_____
Address
_____

_____
Telephone Number

_____
Date

Signature(s) of Debtor(s) (Corporation/Partnership)

I declare under penalty of perjury that the information provided in this petition is true and correct, and that I have been authorized to file this petition on behalf of the debtor.

If debtor is a corporation filing under chapter 11, United States Code, specified in this petition.

X_____
Signature of Authorized Individual

_____
Print or Type Name of Authorized Individual

_____
Title of Authorized Individual by Debtor to File this Petition

_____
Date

EXHIBIT A

(To be completed if debtor is required to file periodic reports (e.g., forms 10K and 10Q) with the Securities and Exchange Commission pursuant to Section 13 or 15(d) of the Securities Exchange Act of 1934 and is requesting relief under chapter 11)

☐ Exhibit A is attached and made part of this petition.

EXHIBIT B

(To be completed if debtor is an individual whose debts are primarily consumer debts)

I, the attorney for the petitioner named in the foregoing petition, declare that I have informed the petitioner that [he or she] may proceed under chapter 7, 11, 12, or 13 of title 11, United States Code, and have explained the relief available under each such chapter.

X_____
Signature of Attorney for Debtor(s)   Date

EXHIBIT C

Does the debtor own or have possession of any property that poses or is alleged to pose a threat of imminent and identifiable harm to public health or safety?

☐ Yes, and Exhibit C is attached and made a part of this petition.
☐ No

Signature of Non-Attorney Petition Preparer

I certify that I am a bankruptcy petition preparer as defined in 11 U.S.C. § 110, that I prepared this document for compensation, and that I have provided the debtor with a copy of this document.

_____
Printed Name of Bankruptcy Petition Preparer

_____
Social Security Number

_____
Address

Names and Social Security numbers of all other Individuals who prepared or assisted in preparing this document:

If more than one person prepared this document, attach additional sheets conforming to the appropriate official form for each person.

X_____
Signature of Bankruptcy Petition Preparer

_____
Date

A bankruptcy petition preparer's failure to comply with the provisions of title 11 and the Federal Rules of Bankruptcy Procedure may result in fines or imprisonment or both 11 U.S.C. § 110; 18 U.S.C. § 156.

Form B1XA, 9-97　　　　　　　**Blumberg**Excelsior, Inc NYC 10013

EXHIBIT "A"

UNITED STATES BANKRUPTCY COURT　　　　**DISTRICT OF**

In re:　　　　　　　　　　　　　　Debtor(s)　　　Case No.
　　　　　　　　　　　　　　　　　　　　　　　Chapter

[If debtor is required to file periodic reports (e.g., forms 10K and 10Q) with the Securities and Exchange Commission pursuant to Section 13 or 15(d) of the Securities Exchange Act of 1934 and is requesting relief under chapter 11 of the Bankruptcy Code, this Exhibit "A" shall be completed and attached to the petition.]

Exhibit "A" to Voluntary Petition

1. If any of debtor's securities are registered under § 12 of the Securities and Exchange Act of 1934, the SEC file number is

2. The following financial data is the latest available information and refers to debtor's condition on

　　a. Total Assets ....$

　　b. Total Liabilities ....

　　c. Debt securities held by more than 500 holders.

Approximate
number of
holders

☐ secured	☐ unsecured	☐ subordinated	$
☐ secured	☐ unsecured	☐ subordinated	
☐ secured	☐ unsecured	☐ subordinated	
☐ secured	☐ unsecured	☐ subordinated	
☐ secured	☐ unsecured	☐ subordinated	

　　d. Number of shares of preferred stock....................................

　　e. Number of shares of common stock ....

Comments, if any:

3. Brief description of debtor's business:

4. List the name of any person who directly or indirectly owns, controls or holds, with power to vote, 5% or more of the voting securities of debtor:

Form 7 Stmt. of Financial
Affairs (9-00)

BlumbergExcelsior, Inc., Publisher nyc 10013
www.blumberg.com

UNITED STATES BANKRUPTCY COURT

DISTRICT OF

In re:

Debtor(s)   *Case No.*

STATEMENT OF FINANCIAL AFFAIRS

This statement is to be completed by every debtor. Spouses filing a joint petition may file a single statement on which the information for both spouses is combined. If the case is filed under chapter 12 or chapter 13, a married debtor must furnish information for both spouses whether or not a joint petition is filed, unless the spouses are separated and a joint petition is not filed. An individual debtor engaged in business as a sole proprietor, partner, family farmer, or self-employed professional, should provide the information requested on this statement concerning all such activities as well as the individual's personal affairs.

Questions 1-18 are to be completed by all debtors. Debtors that are or have been in business, as defined below, also must complete Questions 19-25. **If the answer to any question is "None," or the question is not applicable, mark the box labeled "None."** If additional space is needed for the answer to any question, use and attach a separate sheet properly identified with the case name, case number (if known), and the number of the question.

DEFINITIONS

"In business." A debtor is "in business" for the purpose of this form if the debtor is a corporation or partnership. An individual debtor is "in business" for the purpose of this form if the debtor is or has been, within the six years immediately preceding the filing of this bankruptcy case, any of the following: an officer, director, managing executive, or person in control of a corporation; a partner, other than a limited partner, of a partnership; a sole proprietor or self-employed.

"Insider." The term "insider" includes but is not limited to: relatives of the debtor; general partners of the debtor and their relatives; corporations of which the debtor is an officer, director, or person in control; officers, directors, and any person in control of a corporate debtor and their relatives; affiliates of the debtor and insiders of such affiliates; any managing agent of the debtor. 11 U.S.C. §101.

☐ None **1. Income from Employment or Operation of Business**

State the gross amount of income the debtor has received from employment, trade, or profession, or from operation of the debtor's business from the beginning of this calendar year to the date this case was commenced. State also the gross amounts received during the **two years** immediately preceding this calendar year. (A debtor that maintains, or has maintained, financial records on the basis of a fiscal rather than a calendar year may report fiscal year income. Identify the beginning and ending dates of the debtor's fiscal year.) If a joint petition is filed, state income for each spouse separately. (Married debtors filing under chapter 12 or chapter 13 must state income of both spouses whether or not a joint petition is filed, unless the spouses are separated and a joint petition is not filed.)
Give AMOUNT and SOURCE (If more than one).

☐ None **2. Income Other than from Employment or Operation of Business**

State the amount of income received by the debtor other than from employment, trade, profession, or operation of the debtor's business during the **two years** immediately preceding the commencement of this case. Give particulars. If a joint petition is filed, state income for each spouse separately. (Married debtors filing under chapter 12 or chapter 13 must state income for each spouse whether or not a joint petition is filed, unless the spouses are separated and a joint petition is not filed.) Give AMOUNT and SOURCE.

3. Payments to Creditors

☐ None a. List all payments on loans, installment purchases of goods or services, and other debts, aggregating more than $600 to any creditor, made within **90 days** immediately preceding the commencement of this case. (Married debtors filing under chapter 12 or chapter 13 must include payments by either or both spouses whether or not a joint petition is filed, unless the spouses are separated and a joint petition is not filed.)
Give NAME AND ADDRESS OF CREDITOR, DATES OF PAYMENTS, AMOUNT PAID and AMOUNT STILL OWING.

☐ None b. List all payments made within **one year** immediately preceding the commencement of this case to or for the benefit of creditors who are or were insiders. (Married debtors filing under chapter 12 or chapter 13 must include payments by either or both spouses whether or not a joint petition is filed, unless the spouses are separated and a joint petition is not filed.)
Give NAME AND ADDRESS OF CREDITOR AND RELATIONSHIP TO DEBTOR, DATE OF PAYMENT, AMOUNT PAID and AMOUNT STILL OWING.

4. Suits and Administrative Proceedings, Executions, Garnishments and Attachments

☐ None a. List all suits and administrative proceedings to which the debtor is or was a party within **one year** immediately preceding the filing of this bankruptcy case. (Married debtors filing under chapter 12 or chapter 13 must include information concerning either or both spouses whether or not a joint petition is filed, unless the spouses are separated and a joint petition is not filed.)
Give CAPTION OF SUIT AND CASE NUMBER, NATURE OF PROCEEDING, COURT OR AGENCY AND LOCATION and STATUS OR DISPOSITION.

☐ None b. Describe all property that has been attached, garnished, or seized under any legal or equitable process within **one year**

Immediately preceding the commencement of this case. (Married debtors filing under chapter 12 or chapter 13 must include information concerning property of either or both spouses whether or not a joint petition is filed, unless the spouses are separated and a joint petition is not filed.)

Give NAME AND ADDRESS OF PERSON FOR WHOSE BENEFIT PROPERTY WAS SEIZED, DATE OF SEIZURE and DESCRIPTION AND VALUE OF PROPERTY.

☐ None　　**5. Repossessions, Foreclosures, and Returns**

List all property that has been repossessed by a creditor, sold at a foreclosure sale, transferred through a deed in lieu of foreclosure or returned to the seller, within one year immediately preceding the commencement of this case. (Married debtors filing under chapter 12 or chapter 13 must include information concerning property o either or both spouses whether or not a joint petition is filed, unless the spouses are separated and a joint petition is not filed.)

Give NAME AND ADDRESS OF CREDITOR OR SELLER, DATE OF REPOSSESSION, FORECLOSURE SALE, TRANSFER OR RETURN and DESCRIPTION AND VALUE OF PROPERTY.

6.Assignments and Receiverships

☐ None　　a. Describe any assignment of property for the benefit of creditors made within 120 days immediately preceding the commencement of this case. (Married debtors filing under chapter 12 or chapter 13 must include any assignment by either or both spouses whether or not a join petition is filed, unless the spouses are separated and a joint petition is not filed.)

Give NAME AND ADDRESS OF ASSIGNEE, DATE OF ASSIGNMENT and TERMS OF ASSIGNMENT OR SETTLEMENT.

☐ None　　b. List all property which has been in the hands of a custodian, receiver, or court-appointed official within one year immediately preceding the commencement of this case. (Married debtors filing under chapter 12 or chapter 13 must include information concerning property of either or both spouses whether or not a joint petition is filed, unless the spouses are separated and a joint petition is not filed.)

Give NAME AND ADDRESS OF CUSTODIAN, NAME AND LOCATION OF OUCRT, CASE TITLE & NUMBER, DATE OF ORDER and DESCRIPTION AND VALUE OF PROPERTY.

☐ None　　**7. Gifts**

List all gifts or charitable contributions made within one year immediately preceding the commencement of this case except ordinary and usual gifts to family members aggregating less the $200 in value per individual family member and charitable contributions aggregating less than $100 per recipient. (Married debtors filing under chapter 12 or chapter 13 must include gifts or contributions by either or both spouses whether or not a joint petition is filed, unless the spouses are separated and a joint petition is not filed.)

Give NAME AND ADDRESS OF PERSON OR ORGANIZATION, RELATIONSHIP TO DEBTOR, IF ANY, DATE OF GIFT, and DESCRIPTION AND VALUE OF GIFT.

☐ None　　**8. Losses**

List all losses from fire, theft, other casualty or gambling within one year immediately preceding the commencement of this case or since the commencement of this case. (Married debtors filing under chater 12 or chapter 13 must include losses by either or both spouses whether or not a joint petition is filed, unless the spouses are separated and a joint petition is not filed.)

Give DESCRIPTION AND VALUE OF PROPERTY, DESCRIPTION OF CIRCUMSTANCES AND, IF LOSS WAS COVERED IN WHOLE OR IN PART BY INSURANCE, GIVE PARTICULARS and DATE OF LOSS.

☐ None　　**9. Payments Related to Debt Counseling or Bankruptcy**

List all payments made or property transferred by or on behalf of the debtor to any persons, including attorneys, for consultation concerning debt consolidation, relief under the bankruptcy law or preparation of a petition in bankruptcy within one year immediately preceding the commencement of this case.

Give NAME AND ADDRESS OF PAYEE, DATE OF PAYMENT, NAME OF PAYER IF OTHER THAN DEBTOR and AMOUNT OF MONEY OR DESCRIPTION AND VALUE OF PROPERTY.

☐ None　　**10. Other Transfers**

List all other property, other than property transferred in the ordinary course of the business or financial affairs of the bebtor, transferred either absolutely or as security within one year immediately preceding the commencement of this case. (Married debtors filing under chapter 12 or chapter 13 must include transfers by either or both spouses whether or not a joint petition is file, unless the souses are separated and a joint petition is not filed.)

Give NAME AND ADDRESS OF TRANSFEREE, RELATIONSHIP TO DEBTOR, DATE, and DESCRIBE PROPERTY TRANSFERRED AND VALUE RECEIVED.

☐ None   **11. Closed Financial Accounts**

List all financial accounts and instruments held in the name of the debtor or for the benefit of the debtor which were closed, sold, or otherwise transferred within one year immediately preceding the commencement of this case. Include checking, savings, or other financial accounts, certificates of deposit, or other instruments; shares and share accounts held in banks, credit unions, pension funds, cooperatives, associations, brokerage houses and other financial institutions. (Married debtors filing under chapter 12 or chapter 13 must include information concerning accounts or instruments held by or for either or both spouses whether or not a joint petition is filed, unless the spouses are separated and a joint petition is not filed.)

Give NAME AND ADDRESS OF INSTITUTION, TYPE AND NUMBER OF ACCOUNT AND AMOUNT OF FINAL BALANCE and AMOUNT AND DATE OF SALE OR CLOSING.

☐ None   **12. Safe Deposit Boxes**

List each safe deposit or other box or depository in which the debtor has or had securities, cash, or other valuables within one year immediately preceding the commencement of this case. (Married debtors filing under chapter 12 or chapter 13 must include depositories of either or both spouses whether or not a joint petition is filed, unless the spouses are separated and a joint petition is not filed.)

Give NAME AND ADDRESS OF BANK OR OTHER DEPOSITORY, NAMES AND ADDRESSES OF THOSE WITH ACCESS TO BOX OR DEPOSITORY, DESCRIPTION OF CONTENTS and DATE OF TRANSFER OR SURRENDER, IF ANY.

☐ None   **13. Setoffs**

List all setoffs made by any creditor, including a bank, against a debt or deposit of the debtor within 90 days preceding the commencement of this case. (Married debtors filing under chapter 12 or chapter 13 must include information concerning either or both spouses whether or not a joint petition is filed, unless the spouses are separated and a joint petition is not filed.)

Give NAME AND ADDRESS OR CREDITOR, DATE OF SETOFF and AMOUNT OF SETOFF.

☐ None   **14. Property Held for Another Person**

List all property owned by another person that the debtor holds or controls.

Give NAME AND ADDRESS OF OWNER, DESCRIPTION AND VALUE OF PROPERTY and LOCATION OF PROPERTY.

☐ None   **15. Prior Address of Debtor**

If the debtor has moved within the two years immediately preceding the commencement of this case, list all premises which the debtor occupied during that period and vacated prior to the commencement of this case. If a joint petition is filed, report also any separate address of either spouse.

Give ADDRESS, NAME USED and DATES OF OCCUPANCY.

☐ None   **16. Spouses and Former Spouses**

If the debtor resides or resided in a community property state, commonwealth, or territory (including Alaska, Arizona, California, Idaho, Louisiana, Nevada, New Mexico, Puerto Rico, Texas, Washington, or Wisconsin) within the six-year period immediately preceding the commencement of the case, identify the name of the debtor's spouse and of any former spouse who resides or resided with the debtor in the community property state.

Give NAME.

☐ None   **17. Environmental Information**

For the purpose of this question, the following definitions apply: "Environmental Law" means any federal, state, or local statute or regulation regulating pollution, contamination, releases of hazardous or toxic substances, wastes or material into the air, land, soil, surface water, groundwater, or other medium, including, but not limited to, statutes or regulations regulating the cleanup of these substances, wastes, or material. "Site" means any location, facility, or property as defined under any Environmental Law, whether or not presently or formerly owned or operated by the debtor, including, but not limited to, disposal sites. "Hazardous Material" means anything defined as a hazardous waste, hazardous substance, toxic substance, hazardous material, pollutant, or contaminant or similar term under an Environmental Law.

☐ None   **a.** List the name and address of every site for which the debtor has received notice in writing by a governmental unit that it may be liable or potentially liable under or in violation of an Environmental law. Indicate the governmental unit, the date of the notice, and, if know, the Environmental Law:

Give SITE NAME AND ADDRESS, NAME AND ADDRESS OF GOVERNMENTAL UNIT, DATE OF NOTICE and ENVIRONMENTAL LAW.

☐ None   **b.** List the name and address of every site for which the debtor has provided notice to a governmental unit of a release of Hazardous Material. Indicate the governmental unit to which the notice was sent and the date of the notice.

Give SITE NAME AND ADDRESS, NAME AND ADDRESS OF GOVERNMENTAL UNIT, DATE OF NOTICE and ENVIRONMENTAL LAW.

☐ None   **c.** List all judicial or administrative proceedings, including settlements or orders, under any Environmental Law with respect to which the debtor is or was a party. Indicate the name and address of the governmental unit that is or was a party to the proceeding, and the docket number.

Give NAME AND ADDRESS OF GOVERNMENTAL UNIT, DOCKET NUMBER and STATUS OR DISPOSITION.

18. Nature, Location and Name of Business

☐ None   **a.** If the debtor is an individual, list the names and addresses of all businesses in which the debtor was an officer, director, partner, or managing executive of a corporation, partnership, sole proprietorship or was a self-employed professional within the two years immediately preceding the commencement of this case, or in which the debtor owned 5 percent or more of the voting or equity securities within the two years immediately preceding the commencement of this case.

b. If the debtor is a partnership, list the names and addresses of all businesses in which the debtor was a partner or owned 5 percent or more of the voting securities, within the two years immediately preceding the commencement of this case.

c. If the debtor is a corporation, list the names and addresses of all businesses in which the debtor was a partner or owned 5 percent or more of the voting securities within the two years immediately preceding the commencement of this case.

Give NAME, ADDRESS, NATURE OF BUSINESS and BEGINNING AND ENDING DATES OF OPERATION.

The following questions are to be completed as shown below.*

19. Books, Records, and Financial Statements

☐ None   a. List all bookkeepers and accountants who within the six years immediately preceding the filing of this bankruptcy case kept or supervised the keeping of books of account and records of the debtor.

Give NAME AND ADDRESS and DATES SERVICE RENDERED.

☐ None   b. List all firms or individuals who within the two years immediately preceding the filing of this bankruptcy case have audited the books of account and records, or prepared a financial statement of the debtor.

Give NAME, ADDRESS and DATES SERVICES RENDERED.

☐ None   c. List all firms or individuals who at the time of the commencement of this case were in possession of the books of account and records of the debtor. If any of the books of account and records are not available, explain.

Give NAME AND ADDRESS and DATE ISSUED.

☐ None   d. List all financial institutions, creditors and other parties, including mercantile and trade agencies, to whom a financial statement was issued within the two years immediately preceding the commencement of this case by the debtor.

Give NAME AND ADDRESS and DATE ISSUED.

20. Inventories

☐ None   a. List the dates of the last two inventories taken of your property, the name of the person who supervised the taking of each inventory, and the dollar amount and basis of each inventory.

Give DATE OF INVENTORY, INVENTORY, SUPERVISOR and DOLLAR AMOUNT OF INVENTORY (specify cost, market or other basis).

☐ None   b. List the name and address of the person having possession of the records of each of the two inventories reported in a., above.

Give DATE OF INVENTORY and NAME AND ADDRESSES OF CUSTODIAN OF INVENTORY RECORDS.

21. Current Partners, Officers, Directors and Shareholders

☐ None   a. If the debtor is a partnership, list the nature and percentage of partnership interest of each member of the partnership.

Give NAME AND ADDRESS, NATURE OR INTEREST and PERCENTAGE OF THE INTEREST.

☐ None   b. If the debtor is a corporation, list all officers and directors of the corporation, and each stockholder who directly or indirectly owns, controls, or holds 5 percent or more of the voting securities of the corporation.

Give NAME AND ADDRESS, TITLE and NATURE AND PERCENTAGE OF STOCK OWNERSHIP.

22. Former Partners, Officers, Directors and Shareholders

☐ None   a. If the debtor is a partnership, list each member who withdrew from the partnership within one year immediately preceding the commencement of this case.

Give NAME, ADDRESS and DATE OF WITHDRAWAL.

☐ None   b. If the debtor is a corporation, list all officers or directors whose relationship with the corporation terminated within one year immediately preceding the commencement of the case.

Give NAME AND ADDRESS, TITLE and DATE OF TERMINATION.

23. Withdrawals from a Partnership or Distributions by a Corporation

☐ None   If the debtor is a partnership or corporation, list all withdrawals or distributions credited or given to an insider, including compensation in any form, bonuses, loans, stock redemption, options exercised and any other perquisite during one year immediately preceding the commencement of this case.

Give NAME & ADDRESS OF RECIPIENT, RELATIONSHIP TO DEBTOR, DATE AND PURPOSE OR WITHDRAWAL, and AMOUNT OF MONEY OR DESCRIPTION AND VALUE OR PROPERTY.

24. Tax Consolidation Group.

☐   If the debtor is a corporation, list the name and federal taxpayer identification number of the parent corporation of any consolidated group for tax purposes of which the debtor has been a member at any time within the six-year period immediately preceding the commencement of the case.

Give NAME OF PARENT CORPORATION and TAXPAYER IDENTIFICATION NUMBER.

25. Pension Funds.

☐   If the debtor is not an individual, list the name and federal taxpayer identification number of any fund to which the debtor, as an employer, has been responsible for contributing at any time within the six-year period immediately preceding the commencement of the case.

Give NAME OF PENSION FUND and TAXPAYER IDENTIFICATION NUMBER.

_____continuation sheets attached

Complete unsworn declaration on page 3076-5

* The following questions are to be completed by every debtor that is a corporation or partnership and by any individual debtor who is or has been, within the six years immediately preceding the commencement of this case, any of the following: an officer, director, managing executive, or owner of more than 5 percent of the voting securities or a corporation; a partner, other than a limited partner, of a partnership; a sole proprietor or otherwise self-employed. (An individual or joint debtor should complete this portion of the statement only if the debtor is or has been in business, as defined above, within the six years immediately preceding the commencement of this case. A debtor who has not been in business within those six years should directly to the signature page.)

[If completed by an individual or individual and spouse]

I declare under penalty of perjury that I have read the answers contained in the foregoing statement of financial affairs and any attachments thereto and that they are true and correct.

Date ————————————————   Signature ————————————————————————
                                        of Debtor

Date ————————————————   Signature ————————————————————————
                                        of Joint Debtor
                                        (if any)

....

[If completed on behalf of a partnership or corporation]

I, declare under penalty of perjury that I have read the answers contained in the foregoing statement of financial affairs and any attachments thereto and that they are true and correct to the best of my knowledge, information and belief.

Date ———————————————   Signature ————————————————————

                                        ————————————————————
                                        Print Name and Title

[An individual signing on behalf of a partnership or corporation must indicate position or relationship to debtor.]

———————— continuation sheets attached.

Penalty for making a false statement: Fine of up to $500,000 or imprisonment for up to 5 years, or both. 18 U.S.C. §§152 and 3571.

....

CERTIFICATION AND SIGNATURE OF NON-ATTORNEY BANKRUPTCY PETITION PREPARER (See 11 U.S.C. § 110)

I certify that I am a bankruptcy petition preparer as defined in 11 U.S.C. § 110, that I prepared this document for compensation, and that I have provided the debtor with a copy of this document.

————————————————————————   ————————————————————
Printed or Typed Name of Bankruptcy Petition Preparer   Social Security No.

————————————————————————

————————————————————————
Address

Names and Social Security numbers of all other individuals who prepared or assisted in preparing this document: If more than one person prepared this document, attach additional signed sheets conforming to the appropriate Official Form for each person.

X ————————————————————————   ————————————————
  Signature of Bankruptcy Petition Preparer   Date

A bankruptcy petition preparer's failure to comply with the provisions of title II and the Federal Rules of Bankruptcy Procedure may result in fines or imprisonment or both. 18 U.S.C. § 156.

Form B6 (6-90)   Julius Blumberg, Inc. NYC 10013

UNITED STATES BANKRUPTCY COURT   DISTRICT OF

In re: _____   Debtor(s)   Case No. _____   (If Known)

See summary below for the list of schedules. Include Unsworn Declaration under Penalty of Perjury at the end.

GENERAL INSTRUCTIONS: Schedules D, E and F have been designed for the listing of each claim only once. Even when a claim is secured only in part, or entitled to priorityonly in part, it still should be listed only once. A claim which is secured in whole or in part should be listed on ScheduleD only, and a claim which is entitled to priority in whole or in part should be listed in Schedule E only. Do not list the same claim twice. If a creditor has more than one claim, such as claims arising from separate transactions, each claim should be scheduled separately.

Review the specific instructions for each schedule before completing the schedule.

SUMMARY OF SCHEDULES

Indicate as to each schedule whether that schedule is attached and state the number of pages in each. Report the totals from Schedules A, B, D, E, F, I and J in the boxes provided. Add the amounts from Schedules A and B to determine the total amount of the debtor's assets. Add the amounts from Schedules D, E, and F to determine the total amount of the debtor's liabilities.

Name of Schedule	Attached (Yes No)	Number of sheets	Assets	Liabilities	Other
A - Real Property					
B - Personal Property					
C - Property Claimed as Exempt					
D - Creditors Holding Secured Claims					
E - Creditors Holding Unsecured Priority Claims					
F - Creditors Holding Unsecured Nonpriority Claims					
G - Executory Contracts and Unexpired Leases					
H - Codebtors					
I - Current Income of Individual Debtor(s)					
J - Current Expenditures of Individual Debtor(s)					
Total Number of Sheets of All Schedules					
Total Assets					
Total Liabilities					

Form B6 A/B, P1(6-90)   Julius Blumberg, Inc. NYC 10013

In re: Debtor(s)   Case No.   (if known)

SCHEDULE A - REAL PROPERTY

DESCRIPTION AND LOCATION OF PROPERTY	NATURE OF DEBTOR'S INTEREST IN PROPERTY	H W J C	CURRENT MARKET VALUE OF DEBTOR'S INTEREST IN PROPERTY WITHOUT DEDUCTING ANY SECURED CLAIM OR EXEMPTION	AMOUNT OF SECURED CLAIM

Total -> $ (Report also on Summary of Schedules.)

SCHEDULE B - PERSONAL PROPERTY

TYPE OF PROPERTY	N O N E	DESCRIPTION AND LOCATION OF PROPERTY	H W J C	CURRENT MARKET VALUE OF DEBTOR'S INTEREST IN PROPERTY WITHOUT DEDUCTING ANY SECURED CLAIM OR EXEMPTION
1. Cash on hand				
2. Checking, savings or other financial accounts, certificates of deposit, or shares in banks, savings and loan, thrift, building and loan, and homestead associations, or credit unions, brokerage houses, or cooperatives.				
3. Security deposits with public utilities, telephone companies, landlords, and others.				
4. Household goods and furnishings including audio, video and computer equipment.				
5. Books; pictures and other art objects; antiques; stamp, coin, record, tape, compact disc, and other collections or collectibles.				
6. Wearing apparel.				
7. Furs and jewelry.				
8. Firearms and sports, photographic, and other hobby equipment.				
9. Interests in insurance policies. Name insurance company of each policy and itemize surrender or refund value of each.				

3072 © 1991 JULIUS BLUMBERG, INC.. NYC 10013

Form B6B, P2 (6-90)   Julius Blumberg, Inc. NYC 10013   **SCHEDULE B**
PERSONAL PROPERTY

In re: Debtor(s)   Case No.   (if known)

TYPE OF PROPERTY	N O N E	DESCRIPTION AND LOCATION OF PROPERTY	H W J C	CURRENT MARKET VALUE OF DEBTOR'S INTEREST IN PROPERTY WITHOUT DEDUCTING ANY SECURED CLAIM OR EXEMPTION
10. Annuities. Itemize and name each issuer.				
11. Interests in IRA, ERISA, Keogh, or other pension or profit sharing plans. Itemize				
12. Stock and interests in incorporated and unincorporated businesses. Itemize.				
13. Interest in partnerships or joint ventures. Itemize.				
14. Government and corporate bonds and other negotiable and nonnegotiable instruments.				
15. Accounts receivable.				
16. Alimony, maintenance, support, and property settlements to which the debtor is or may be entitled. Give particulars.				
17. Other liquidated debts owing debtor including tax refunds. Give particulars.				
18. Equitable or future interests, life estates, and rights or powers exercisable for the benefit of the debtor other than those listed in Schedule of Real Property.				
19. Contingent and noncontingent interests in estate of a decedent, death benefit plan, life insurance policy, or trust.				
20. Other contingent and unliquidated claims of every nature, including tax refunds, counterclaims of the debtor, and rights to setoff claims. Give estimated value of each.				
21. Patents, copyrights, and other intellectual property. Give particulars.				
22. Licenses, franchises, and other general intangibles. Give particulars.				
23. Automobiles, trucks, trailers, and other vehicles and accessories.				
24. Boats, motors, and accessories.				
25. Aircraft and accessories.				
26. Office equipment, furnishings, and supplies.				
27. Machinery, fixtures, equipment, and supplies used in business.				
28. Inventory.				
29. Animals.				
30. Crops - growing or harvested. Give particulars.				
31. Farming equipment and implements.				
32. Farm supplies, chemicals, and feed.				
33. Other personal property of any kind not already listed. Itemize.				

(Include amounts from any continuation sheets attached. Report total also on Summary of Schedules)   Total -> | $

_____ continuation sheets attached

3072 © 1991 JULIUS BLUMBERG, INC., NYC 10013

Form B6 C (6,90)

Julius Blumberg, Inc. NYC 10013

In re:

                      Debtor(s)   Case No.   (if known)

SCHEDULE C - PROPERTY CLAIMED AS EXEMPT

Debtor elects the exemptions to which debtor is entitled under (Check one box)

☐ 11 U.S.C. § 522(b)(1): Exemptions provided in 11 U.S.C. § 522(d). Note: These exemptions are available only in certain states.

☐ 11 U.S.C. § 522(b)(2): Exemptions available under applicable nonbankruptcy federal laws, state or local law.

DESCRIPTION OF PROPERTY	SPECIFY LAW PROVIDING EACH EXEMPTION	VALUE OF CLAIMED EXEMPTION	CURRENT MARKET VALUE OF PROPERTY WITHOUT DEDUCTING EXEMPTION

3072 © 1991 JULIUS BLUMBERG. INC.. NYC 10013

Form B6 D (6-90)   Julius Blumberg, Inc. NYC 10013

In re: _____   Debtor(s)   Case No. _____   (if known)

SCHEDULE D - CREDITORS HOLDING SECURED CLAIMS

☐ Check this box if debtor has no creditors holding secured claims to report on this Schedule D.

CREDITOR'S NAME AND MAILING ADDRESS INCLUDING ZIP CODE	CO D E B T	H W J C	DATE CLAIM WAS INCURRED, NATURE OF LIEN, AND DESCRIPTION AND MARKET VALUE OF PROPERTY SUBJECT TO LIEN	C U D *	AMOUNT OF CLAIM WITHOUT DEDUCTING VALUE OF COLLATERAL	UNSECURED PORTION IF ANY
A/C #						
			VALUE $			
A/C #						
			VALUE $			
A/C #						
			VALUE $			
A/C #						
			VALUE $			
A/C #						
			VALUE $			
A/C #						
			VALUE $			
A/C #						
			VALUE $			
A/C #						
			VALUE $			
A/C #						
			VALUE $			

Subtotal -> (Total of this page) $ _____

Total -> (use only on last page) $ _____

_____ continuation sheets attached

*If contingent, enter C; if unliquidated, enter U; if disputed, enter D.

(Report total also on Summary of Schedules)

Form B6 E (4/98)

BlumbergExcelsior Inc. NYC 10013

In re: _____ Debtor(s)   Case No. _____ (if known)

SCHEDULE E - CREDITORS HOLDING UNSECURED PRIORITY CLAIMS

☐ Check this box if debtor has no creditors holding unsecured priority claims to report on this Schedule E

TYPE OF PRIORITY CLAIMS (Check the appropriate box(es) below if claims in that category are listed on the attached sheets)

☐ **Extensions of credit in an involuntary case**   Claims arising in the ordinary course of the debtor's business or financial affairs after the commencement of the case but before the earlier of the appointment of a trustee or the order for relief. 11 U.S.C. § 507 (a) (2).

☐ **Wages, salaries, and commissions**   Wages, salaries, and commissions, including vacation, severance, and sick leave pay owing to employees, and commissions owing to qualifying independent sales representatives up to $4,300* per person, earned within 90 days immediately preceding the filing of the original petition, or the cessation of business, whichever occurred first, to the extent provided in 11 U.S.C. § 507 (a) (3).

☐ **Contributions to employee benefit plans**   Money owed to employee benefit plans for services rendered within 180 days immediately preceding the filing of the original petition, or the cessation of business, whichever occurred first, to the extent provided in 11 U.S.C. § 507 (a) (4).

☐ **Certain farmers and fishermen**   Claims of certain farmers and fishermen, up to $4,300* per farmer or fisherman, against the debtor, as provided in 11 U.S.C. § 507 (a) (5).

☐ **Deposits by individuals**   Claims of individuals up to $1,950* for deposits for the purchase, lease, or rental of property or services for personal, family, or household use, that were not delivered or provided. 11 U.S.C. § 507 (a) (6).

☐ **Alimony, Maintenance, or Support**   Claims of a spouse, former spouse, or child of the debtor for alimony, maintenance, or support, to the extent provided in 11 U.S.C. § 507 (a) (7).

☐ **Taxes and Certain Other Debts Owed to Governmental Units**   Taxes, customs duties, and penalties owing to federal, state, and local governmental units as set forth in 11 U.S.C. § 507 (a) (8).

☐ **Commitments to Maintain the Capital of an Insured Depository Institution**   Claims based on commitments to the FDIC, RTC, Director of the Office of Thrift Supervision, Comptroller of the Currency, or Board of Governors of the Federal Reserve System, or their predecessors or successors, to maintain the capital of an insured depository institution. 11 U.S.C. § 507 (a) (9).

*Amounts are subject to adjustment on April 1, 1998, and every three years thereafter with respect to cases commenced on or after the date of adjustment.

CREDITOR'S NAME AND MAILING ADDRESS INCLUDING ZIP CODE	CO DEBT	H W J C	DATE CLAIM WAS INCURRED AND CONSIDERATION FOR CLAIM	C U D *	TOTAL AMOUNT OF CLAIM	AMOUNT ENTITLED TO PRIORITY
A/C#						
A/C#						
A/C#						
A/C#						
A/C#						

Subtotal -> (Total of this page) $ _____

_____ Continuation sheets attached.

Total -> (use only on last page of the completed Schedule E) $ _____

* If contingent, enter C; if unliquidated., enter U; if disputed , enter D.

(Report total also on Summary of Schedules)

3072© 1991 JULIUS BLUMBERG, INC., NYC 10013

Blumbergs Law Products   Form B6 E Cont. (6-90)   Julius Blumberg, Inc. NYC 10013

In re: _____   Debtor(s)   Case No. _____   (if known)

SCHEDULE E - CREDITORS HOLDING UNSECURED PRIORITY CLAIMS
(Continuation Sheet)

CREDITOR'S NAME AND MAILING ADDRESS INCLUDING ZIP CODE	CO D E B T	H W J C	DATE CLAIM WAS INCURRED AND CONSIDERATION FOR CLAIM	C U D *	TOTAL AMOUNT OF CLAIM	AMOUNT ENTITLED TO PRIORITY
A/C #						
A/C #						
A/C #						
A/C #						
A/C #						
A/C #						
A/C #						
A/C #						
A/C #						

Sheet no. _____ attached to Schedule of Creditors
Holding Priority Claims.

Subtotal -> $
(Total of this page)

Total -> $
(use only on last page of completed Schedule E.)

*If contingent, enter C; if unliquidated, enter U; if disputed, enter D.

(Report total also on Summary of Schedules)

3072 © 1991 JULIUS BLUMBERG, INC., NYC 10013

Form B6 F, 9-97

BlumbergExcelsior, Inc NYC 10013

In re: _____ Debtor(s)   Case No. _____ (if known)

SCHEDULE F - CREDITORS HOLDING UNSECURED NONPRIORITY CLAIMS

☐ Check this box if debtor has no creditors holding unsecured nonpriority claims to report on this Schedule F

CREDITOR'S NAME AND MAILING ADDRESS INCLUDING ZIP CODE	CODEBTOR	H W J C.*	DATE CLAIM WAS INCURRED AND CONSIDERATION FOR CLAIM. IF CLAIM IS SUBJECT TO SETOFF, SO STATE.	C U D.**	AMOUNT OF CLAIM
A/C #					
A/C #					
A/C #					
A/C #					
A/C #					
A/C #					
A/C #					
A/C #					
A/C #					

_____ Continuation Sheets attached.

Subtotal -> $ _____
(Total of this page)

Total -> $ _____
(use only on last page of completed Schedule F.)

* If husband, enter H; if wife, enter W; if joint enter J, if community, enter C.

** If contingent, enter C; if unliquidated, enter U; if disputed, enter D.

3072 © 1997 JULIUS BLUMBERG, INC., NYC 10013

Form B6 F Cont., 9-97   BlumbergExcelsior, Inc NYC 10013

In re: Debtor(s)   Case No.   (if known)

SCHEDULE F - CREDITORS HOLDING UNSECURED NONPRIORITY CLAIMS
(Continuation Sheet)

CREDITOR'S NAME AND MAILING ADDRESS INCLUDING ZIP CODE	CODEBTOR	H W J C.	DATE CLAIM WAS INCURRED AND CONSIDERATION FOR CLAIM. IF CLAIM IS SUBJECT TO SETOFF, SO STATE.	C U D **	AMOUNT OF CLAIM
A/C #					
A/C #					
A/C #					
A/C #					
A/C #					
A/C #					
A/C #					
A/C #					
A/C #					

Sheet no. _____ of _____ sheets attached to Schedule of Creditors Holding Nonpriority Claims.

Subtotal -> $

(Total of this page)

Total -> $

(use only on last page of completed Schedule F.)

* If husband, enter H; if wife, enter W; if joint enter J, if community, enter C.

** If contingent, enter C; if unliquidated, enter U; if disputed, enter D.

3072 © 1997 JULIUS BLUMBERG, INC., NYC 10013

Form B6 G (6-90)   Julius Blumberg, Inc. NYC 10013

In re: Debtor(s)   Case No.   (if known)

SCHEDULE G - EXECUTORY CONTRACTS AND UNEXPIRED LEASES

☐ Check this box if debtor has no executory contracts or unexpired leases.

NAME AND MAILING ADDRESS, INCLUDING ZIP CODE, OF OTHER PARTIES TO LEASE OR CONTRACT.	DESCRIPTION OF CONTRACT OR LEASE AND NATURE OF DEBTOR'S INTEREST. STATE WHETHER LEASE IS FOR NONRESIDENTIAL REAL PROPERTY. STATE CONTRACT NUMBER OF ANY GOVERNMENT CONTRACT.

Form B6 H, (6-90)   Julius Blumberg, Inc. NYC 10013

In re: Debtor(s)   Case No.   (if known)

SCHEDULE H - CODEBTORS

☐ Check this box if debtor has no codebtors.

NAME AND ADDRESS OF CODEBTOR	NAME AND ADDRESS OF CREDITOR

3072 © 1991 JULIUS BLUMBERG, INC., NYC 10013

Form B6 Cont. (12/94)   Julius Blumberg, Inc. NYC 10013

In re: _____   Debtor(s)   Case No. _____

(if known)

DECLARATION CONCERNING DEBTOR'S SCHEDULES

DECLARATION UNDER PENALTY OF PERJURY BY INDIVIDUAL DEBTOR

I declare under penalty of perjury that I have read the foregoing summary and schedules, consisting of ——————————— sheets,
(Total shown on summary page plus 1.)
and that they are true and correct to the best of my knowledge, information, and belief.

Date _____   Signature: _____
Debtor

Date _____   Signature: _____
(Joint Debtor, if any) (If joint case, both spouses must sign.)

CERTIFICATION AND SIGNATURE OF NON-ATTORNEY BANKRUPTCY PETITION PREPARER (SEE 11 U.S.C. § 110)

I certify that I am a bankruptcy petition preparer as defined in 11 U.S.C. § 110, that I prepared this document for compensation, and that I have provided the debtor with a copy of this document.

_____   _____
Printed or Typed Name of Bankruptcy Petition Preparer   Social Security No.

_____
Address

Names and Social Security numbers of all other individuals who prepared or assisted in preparing this document:

If more than one person prepared this document, attach additional signed sheets conforming to the appropriate Official Form for each person.

X _____   _____
Signature of Bankruptcy Petition Preparer   Date

A bankruptcy petition preparer's failure to comply with the provisions of title 11 and the Federal Rules of Bankruptcy Procedure may result in fines or imprisonment or both. 11 U.S.C. § 110; 18 U.S.C. § 156

DECLARATION UNDER PENALTY OF PERJURY ON BEHALF OF A CORPORATION OR PARTNERSHIP

I, the ——————————————————— (the president or other officer or an authorized agent of the corporation or a member or an authorized agent of the partnership) of the ————————————————————(corporation or partnership) named as debtor in this case, declare under penalty of perjury that I have read the foregoing summary and schedules, consisting of ———————————————sheets, and that they are true and correct to the best of my knowledge, information, and belief.   (Total shown on summary page plus 1.)

Date _____   Signature: _____
(Print or type name of individual signing on behalf of debtor.)

(An individual signing on behalf of a partnership or corporation must indicate position or relationship to debtor.)

3085   Statement of compensation: Rule 2016(b), 8-91

UNITED STATES BANKRUPTCY COURT   **DISTRICT OF**

In re   Debtor(s)   Case No.   (If Known)

STATEMENT
Pursuant to Rule 2016(b)

The undersigned, pursuant to Rule 2016(b) Bankruptcy Rules, states that:

(1) The undersigned is the attorney for the debtor(s) in this case.
(2) The compensation paid or agreed to be paid by the debtor(s) to the undersigned is:
   (a) for legal services rendered or to be rendered in contemplation of and in connection
        with this case $ ....
   (b) prior to filing this statement, debtor(s) have paid $ ....
   (c) the unpaid balance due and payable is $ ....
(3) $ of the filing fee in this case has been paid.
(4) The services rendered or to be rendered include the following:
   (a) analysis of the financial situation, and rendering advice and assistance to the debtor(s) in determining whether to file a
        petition under title 11 of the United States Code.
   (b) preparation and filing of the petition, schedules, statement of affairs and other documents required by the court.
   (c) representation of the debtor(s) at the meeting of creditors.

(5) The source of payments made by the debtor(s) to the undersigned was from earnings, wages and compensation for services
     performed, and

(6) The source of payments to be made by the debtor(s) to the undersigned for the unpaid balance remaining, if any, will be from
     earnings, wages and compensation for services performed, and

(7) The undersigned has received no transfer, assignment or pledge of property execept the following for the value stated:

(8) The undersigned has not shared or agreed to share with any other entity, other than with members of undersigned's law firm,
     any compensation paid or to be paid except as follows:

Dated: Respectfully submitted, ...*Attorney for Petitioner*

Attorney's name and address ....

Blumbergs Law Products   Form B4 (6-90)   Julius Blumberg, Inc. NYC 10013

UNITED STATES BANKRUPTCY COURT   DISTRICT OF

In re: Debtor(s)   Case No.   (If Known)

LIST OF CREDITORS HOLDING 20 LARGEST UNSECURED CLAIMS

Following is the list of the debtor's creditors holding the 20 largest unsecured claims. The list is prepared in accordance with Fed. R. Bankr. P. 1007(d) for filing in this chapter 11 [or chapter 9] case. The list does not include (1) persons who come within the definition of "insider" set forth in 11 U.S.C. § 101(30), or (2) secured creditors unless the value of the collateral is such that the unsecured deficiency places the creditor among the holders of the 20 largest unsecured claims

(1) NAME OF CREDITOR AND COMPLETE MAILING ADDRESS INCLUDING ZIP CODE	(2) NAME, TELEPHONE NUMBER AND COMPLETE MAILING ADDRESS, INCLUDING ZIP CODE OF EMPLOYEE, AGENT, OR DEPARTMENT OF CREDITOR FAMILIAR WITH CLAIM.	(3) NATURE OF CLAIM (trade debt, bank loan, government contract, etc)	(4) C U D S	(5) AMOUNT OF CLAIM (If secured also state value of security)

"(4) C U D S"   If contingent, enter C; if unliquidated, enter U; if disputed, enter D; if subject to setoff, enter S.

Form B4 (6-90)   Julius Blumberg, Inc. NYC 10013

LIST OF CREDITORS HOLDING 20 LARGEST UNSECURED CLAIMS (continuation)

(1)	(2)	(3)	(4)	(5)

Unsworn Declaration under Penalty of Perjury (partnership or corporation) I declare under penalty of perjury that I have read the answers contained in the foregoing list of creditors and that they are true and corrrect to the best of my knowledge, information and belief.

_____   _____   _____
   Date   Signature   Print Name and Title

(An individual signing on behalf of a partnership or corporation must indicate position or relationship to debtor.)

Penalty for making a false statement: Fine of up to $500.00 or imprisonment for up to 5 years, or both. 18 U.S.C. § § 152 and 3571

3087   Equity security holders list, chapter 11, 8-91

UNITED STATES BANKRUPTCY COURT   **DISTRICT OF**

In re   Debtor(s)   Case No.   (If Known)

LIST OF EQUITY SECURITY HOLDERS

Registered name of holder of security Last know address or place business	Class of security	Number registered	Kind of interest registered

B

Sample Chapter 7 Bankruptcy Forms

These forms may be purchased from BlumbergExcelsior, Inc., or any of its dealers. Reproduction prohibited.

Blumbergs Law Products Official Form B1, P1, 9-97   **Blumberg**Excelsior, Inc NYC 10013

United States Bankruptcy Court **District of**	**Voluntary Petition**
Name of Debtor (If individual, enter Last, First, Middle):	Name of Joint Debtor (Spouse) (Last, First, Middle):
All Other Names used by the debtor in the last 6 years (include married, maiden and trade names):	All Other Names used by the joint debtor in the last 6 years (include married, maiden and trade names):
Soc. Sec./Tax I.D. No. (If more than one, state all):	Soc. Sec./Tax I.D. No. (If more than one, state all):
Street Address of Debtor (No. and street, city, state, zip):	Street Address of Joint Debtor (No. and street, city, state, zip):
County of Residence or Principal Place of Business:	County of Residence or Principal Place of Business:
Mailing Address of Debtor (If different from street address):	Mailing Address of Joint Debtor (If different from street address):

Location of Principal Assets of Business Debtor
(If different from addresses listed above)

Information Regarding Debtor (Check the Applicable Boxes)

Venue (Check any applicable box)
☐ Debtor has been domiciled or has had a residence, principal place of business or principal assets in this District for 180 days immediately preceding the date of this petition or for a longer part of such 180 days than in any other District.
☐ There is a bankruptcy case concerning debtor's affiliate, general partner or partnership pending in this district

Type of Debtor (Check all boxes that apply)		**Chapter or Section of Bankruptcy Code Under Which** **the Pertition is Filed** (Check one box)
☐ Individual	☐ Railroad	
☐ Corporation	☐ Stockbroker	☐ Chapter 7 ☐ Chapter 11 ☐ Chapter 13
☐ Partnership	☐ Commodity Broker	☐ Chapter 9 ☐ Chapter 12
☐ Other		☐ § 304-Case ancillary to foreign proceeding.

Nature of Debt (Check one box)
☐ Consumer/Non-Business ☐ Business

Chapter 11 Small Business (Check all boxes that apply)
☐ Debtor is a small business as defined in 11 U.S.C. § 101.
☐ Debtor is and elects to be considered a small business under 11 U.S.C. § 1121(e) (Optional)

Filing Fee (Check one box)
☐ Full Filing Fee attached.
☐ Filing Fee to be paid in installments (Applicable to individuals only)

Must attach signed application for the court's consideration certifying that the debtor is unable to pay fee except in installments. Rule 1006(b). See Official Form No. 3

Statistical/Administrative Information (Estimates Only)
☐ Debtor estimates that funds will be available for distribution to unsecured creditors.
☐ Debtor estimates that, after any exempt property is excluded and administrative expenses paid, there will be no funds available for distribution to unsecured creditors.

THIS SPACE FOR COURT USE ONLY

Estimated Number of Creditors	1-15	16-49	50-99	100-199	200-999	1000-over
	☐	☐	☐	☐	☐	☐

Estimated Assets						
$0 to $50,000	$50,001 to $100,000	$100,001 to $500,000	$500,001 to $1 million	$1,000,001 to $10 million	$10,000.001 to $100 million	More than $100 million
☐	☐	☐	☐	☐	☐	☐

Estimated Debts						
$0 to $50,000	$50,001 to $100,000	$100,001 to $500,000	$500,001 to $1 million	$1,000,001 to $10 million	$10,000.001 to $100 million	More than $100 million
☐	☐	☐	☐	☐	☐	☐

Official Form B1, P2, 9-01   **Blumberg**Excelsior, Inc NYC 10013

Voluntary Petition
(This page must be completed and filed in every case)

	Name of Debtor(s):

Prior Bankruptcy Case Filed Within Last 6 Years (If more than one, attach additional sheet)

Location Where Filed:	Case Number:	Date Filed:

Pending Bankruptcy Case Filed by any Spouse, Partner, or Affiliate of this Debtor (If more than one, attach additional sheet.)

Name of Debtor:	Case Number:	Date Filed:
District:	Relationship:	Judge:

Signatures

Signature(s) of Debtor(s) (Individual/Joint)

I declare under penalty of perjury that the information provided in this petition is true and correct.

[If petitioner is an individual whose debts are primarily consumer debts and has chosen to file under chapter 7] I am aware that I may proceed under chapter 7, 11,12,13 of title 11, United States Code, understand the relief available under each such chapter, and choose to proceed under chapter 7.

I request relief in accordance with the chapter of title 11, United States Code, specified in this petition.

X_____
Signature of Debtor

X_____
Signature of Joint Debtor

_____
Telephone (If not represented by attorney)

_____
Date

Signature of Attorney

X_____
Signature of Attorney for Debtor(s)

_____
Printed Name of Attorney for Debtor(s)

_____
Firm Name

_____
Address

_____

_____
Telephone Number

_____
Date

Signature(s) of Debtor(s) (Corporation/Partnership)

I declare under penalty of perjury that the information provided in this petition is true and correct, and that I have been authorized to file this petition on behalf of the debtor.

If debtor is a corporation filing under chapter 11, United States Code, specified in this petition.

X_____
Signature of Authorized Individual

_____
Print or Type Name of Authorized Individual

_____
Title of Authorized Individual by Debtor to File this Petition

_____
Date

EXHIBIT A

(To be completed if debtor is required to file periodic reports (e.g., forms 10K and 10Q) with the Securities and Exchange Commission pursuant to Section 13 or 15(d) of the Securities Exchange Act of 1934 and is requesting relief under chapter 11)

☐ Exhibit A is attached and made part of this petition.

EXHIBIT B

(To be completed if debtor is an individual whose debts are primarily consumer debts)

I, the attorney for the petitioner named in the foregoing petition, declare that I have informed the petitioner that [he or she] may proceed under chapter 7, 11, 12, or 13 of title 11, United States Code, and have explained the relief available under each such chapter.

X_____
Signature of Attorney for Debtor(s)   Date

EXHIBIT C

Does the debtor own or have possession of any property that poses or is alleged to pose a threat of imminent and identifiable harm to public health or safety?

☐ Yes, and Exhibit C is attached and made a part of this petition.
☐ No

Signature of Non-Attorney Petition Preparer

I certify that I am a bankruptcy petition preparer as defined in 11 U.S.C. § 110, that I prepared this document for compensation, and that I have provided the debtor with a copy of this document.

_____
Printed Name of Bankruptcy Petition Preparer

_____
Social Security Number

_____
Address

Names and Social Security numbers of all other Individuals who prepared or assisted in preparing this document:

If more than one person prepared this document, attach additional sheets conforming to the appropriate official form for each person.

X_____
Signature of Bankruptcy Petition Preparer

_____
Date

A bankruptcy petition preparer's failure to comply with the provisions of title 11 and the Federal Rules of Bankruptcy Procedure may result in fines or imprisonment or both 11 U.S.C. § 110; 18 U.S.C. § 156.

Blumbergs Law Products • Form 7 Stmt. of Financial Affairs (9-00)

BlumbergExcelsior, Inc., Publisher nyc 10013
www.blumberg.com

UNITED STATES BANKRUPTCY COURT

DISTRICT OF

In re:

Debtor(s)   *Case No.*

STATEMENT OF FINANCIAL AFFAIRS

This statement is to be completed by every debtor. Spouses filing a joint petition may file a single statement on which the information for both spouses is combined. If the case is filed under chapter 12 or chapter 13, a married debtor must furnish information for both spouses whether or not a joint petition is filed, unless the spouses are separated and a joint petition is not filed. An individual debtor engaged in business as a sole proprietor, partner, family farmer, or self-employed professional, should provide the information requested on this statement concerning all such activities as well as the individual's personal affairs.

Questions 1-18 are to be completed by all debtors. Debtors that are or have been in business, as defined below, also must complete Questions 19-25. **If the answer to any question is "None," or the question is not applicable, mark the box labeled "None."** If additional space is needed for the answer to any question, use and attach a separate sheet properly identified with the case name, case number (if known), and the number of the question.

DEFINITIONS

"In business." A debtor is "in business" for the purpose of this form if the debtor is a corporation or partnership. An individual debtor is "in business" for the purpose of this form if the debtor is or has been, within the six years immediately preceding the filing of this bankruptcy case, any of the following: an officer, director, managing executive, or person in control of a corporation; a partner, other than a limited partner, of a partnership; a sole proprietor or self-employed.

"Insider." The term "insider" includes but is not limited to: relatives of the debtor; general partners of the debtor and their relatives; corporations of which the debtor is an officer, director, or person in control; officers, directors, and any person in control of a corporate debtor and their relatives; affiliates of the debtor and insiders of such affiliates; any managing agent of the debtor. 11 U.S.C. §101.

☐ None   **1. Income from Employment or Operation of Business**

State the gross amount of income the debtor has received from employment, trade, or profession, or from operation of the debtor's business from the beginning of this calendar year to the date this case was commenced. State also the gross amounts received during the **two years** immediately preceding this calendar year. (A debtor that maintains, or has maintained, financial records on the basis of a fiscal rather than a calendar year may report fiscal year income. Identify the beginning and ending dates of the debtor's fiscal year.) If a joint petition is filed, state income for each spouse separately. (Married debtors filing under chapter 12 or chapter 13 must state income of both spouses whether or not a joint petition is filed, unless the spouses are separated and a joint petition is not filed.)
Give AMOUNT and SOURCE (If more than one).

☐ None   **2. Income Other than from Employment or Operation of Business**

State the amount of income received by the debtor other than from employment, trade, profession, or operation of the debtor's business during the **two years** immediately preceding the commencement of this case. Give particulars. If a joint petition is filed, state income for each spouse separately. (Married debtors filing under chapter 12 or chapter 13 must state income for each spouse whether or not a joint petition is filed, unless the spouses are separated and a joint petition is not filed.) Give AMOUNT and SOURCE.

3. Payments to Creditors

☐ None   a. List all payments on loans, installment purchases of goods or services, and other debts, aggregating more than $600 to any creditor, made within **90 days** immediately preceding the commencement of this case. (Married debtors filing under chapter 12 or chapter 13 must include payments by either or both spouses whether or not a joint petition is filed, unless the spouses are separated and a joint petition is not filed.)
Give NAME AND ADDRESS OF CREDITOR, DATES OF PAYMENTS, AMOUNT PAID and AMOUNT STILL OWING.

☐ None   b. List all payments made within **one year** immediately preceding the commencement of this case to or for the benefit of creditors who are or were insiders. (Married debtors filing under chapter 12 or chapter 13 must include payments by either or both spouses whether or not a joint petition is filed, unless the spouses are separated and a joint petition is not filed.)
Give NAME AND ADDRESS OF CREDITOR AND RELATIONSHIP TO DEBTOR, DATE OF PAYMENT, AMOUNT PAID and AMOUNT STILL OWING.

4. Suits and Administrative Proceedings, Executions, Garnishments and Attachments

☐ None   a. List all suits and administrative proceedings to which the debtor is or was a party within **one year** immediately preceding the filing of this bankruptcy case. (Married debtors filing under chapter 12 or chapter 13 must include information concerning either or both spouses whether or not a joint petition is filed, unless the spouses are separated and a joint petition is not filed.)
Give CAPTION OF SUIT AND CASE NUMBER, NATURE OF PROCEEDING, COURT OR AGENCY AND LOCATION and STATUS OR DISPOSITION.

☐ None   b. Describe all property that has been attached, garnished, or seized under any legal or equitable process within **one year**

Immediately preceding the commencement of this case. (Married debtors filing under chapter 12 or chapter 13 must include information concerning property of either or both spouses whether or not a joint petition is filed, unless the spouses are separated and a joint petition is not filed.)

Give NAME AND ADDRESS OF PERSON FOR WHOSE BENEFIT PROPERTY WAS SEIZED, DATE OF SEIZURE and DESCRIPTION AND VALUE OF PROPERTY.

☐ None   **5. Repossessions, Foreclosures, and Returns**

List all property that has been repossessed by a creditor, sold at a foreclosure sale, transferred through a deed in lieu of foreclosure or returned to the seller, within one year immediately preceding the commencement of this case. (Married debtors filing under chapter 12 or chapter 13 must include information concerning property o either or both spouses whether or not a joint petition is filed, unless the spouses are separated and a joint petition is not filed.)

Give NAME AND ADDRESS OF CREDITOR OR SELLER, DATE OF REPOSSESSION, FORECLOSURE SALE, TRANSFER OR RETURN and DESCRIPTION AND VALUE OF PROPERTY.

6. Assignments and Receiverships

☐ None   a. Describe any assignment of property for the benefit of creditors made within 120 days immediately preceding the commencement of this case. (Married debtors filing under chapter 12 or chapter 13 must include any assignment by either or both spouses whether or not a join petition is filed, unless the spouses are separated and a joint petition is not filed.)

Give NAME AND ADDRESS OF ASSIGNEE, DATE OF ASSIGNMENT and TERMS OF ASSIGNMENT OR SETTLEMENT.

☐ None   b. List all property which has been in the hands of a custodian, receiver, or court-appointed official within one year immediately preceding the commencement of this case. (Married debtors filing under chapter 12 or chapter 13 must include information concerning property of either or both spouses whether or not a joint petition is filed, unless the spouses are separated and a joint petition is not filed.)

Give NAME AND ADDRESS OF CUSTODIAN, NAME AND LOCATION OF OUCRT, CASE TITLE & NUMBER, DATE OF ORDER and DESCRIPTION AND VALUE OF PROPERTY.

☐ None   **7. Gifts**

List all gifts or charitable contributions made within one year immediately preceding the commencement of this case except ordinary and usual gifts to family members aggregating less the $200 in value per individual family member and charitable contributions aggregating less than $100 per recipient. (Married debtors filing under chapter 12 or chapter 13 must include gifts or contributions by either or both spouses whether or not a joint petition is filed, unless the spouses are separated and a joint petition is not filed.)

Give NAME AND ADDRESS OF PERSON OR ORGANIZATION, RELATIONSHIP TO DEBTOR, IF ANY, DATE OF GIFT, and DESCRIPTION AND VALUE OF GIFT.

☐ None   **8. Losses**

List all losses from fire, theft, other casualty or gambling within one year immediately preceding the commencement of this case or since the commencement of this case. (Married debtors filing under chater 12 or chapter 13 must include losses by either or both spouses whether or not a joint petition is filed, unless the spouses are separated and a joint petition is not filed.)

Give DESCRIPTION AND VALUE OF PROPERTY, DESCRIPTION OF CIRCUMSTANCES AND, IF LOSS WAS COVERED IN WHOLE OR IN PART BY INSURANCE, GIVE PARTICULARS and DATE OF LOSS.

☐ None   **9. Payments Related to Debt Counseling or Bankruptcy**

List all payments made or property transferred by or on behalf of the debtor to any persons, including attorneys, for consultation concerning debt consolidation, relief under the bankruptcy law or preparation of a petition in bankruptcy within one year immediately preceding the commencement of this case.

Give NAME AND ADDRESS OF PAYEE, DATE OF PAYMENT, NAME OF PAYER IF OTHER THAN DEBTOR and AMOUNT OF MONEY OR DESCRIPTION AND VALUE OF PROPERTY.

☐ None   **10. Other Transfers**

List all other property, other than property transferred in the ordinary course of the business or financial affairs of the bebtor, transferred either absolutely or as security within one year immediately preceding the commencement of this case. (Married debtors filing under chapter 12 or chapter 13 must include transfers by either or both spouses whether or not a joint petition is file, unless the souses are separated and a joint petition is not filed.)

Give NAME AND ADDRESS OF TRANSFEREE, RELATIONSHIP TO DEBTOR, DATE, and DESCRIBE PROPERTY TRANSFERRED AND VALUE RECEIVED.

☐ None   **11. Closed Financial Accounts**

List all financial accounts and instruments held in the name of the debtor or for the benefit of the debtor which were closed, sold, or otherwise transferred within one year immediately preceding the commencement of this case. Include checking, savings, or other financial accounts, certificates of deposit, or other instruments; shares and share accounts held in banks, credit unions, pension funds, cooperatives, associations, brokerage houses and other financial institutions. (Married debtors filing under chapter 12 or chapter 13 must include information concerning accounts or instruments held by or for either or both spouses whether or not a joint petition is filed, unless the spouses are separated and a joint petition is not filed.)

Give NAME AND ADDRESS OF INSTITUTION, TYPE AND NUMBER OF ACCOUNT AND AMOUNT OF FINAL BALANCE and AMOUNT AND DATE OF SALE OR CLOSING.

☐ None   **12. Safe Deposit Boxes**

List each safe deposit or other box or depository in which the debtor has or had securities, cash, or other valuables within one year immediately preceding the commencement of this case. (Married debtors filing under chapter 12 or chapter 13 must include depositories of either or both spouses whether or not a joint petition is filed, unless the spouses are separated and a joint petition is not filed.)

Give NAME AND ADDRESS OF BANK OR OTHER DEPOSITORY, NAMES AND ADDRESSES OF THOSE WITH ACCESS TO BOX OR DEPOSITORY, DESCRIPTION OF CONTENTS and DATE OF TRANSFER OR SURRENDER, IF ANY.

☐ None   **13. Setoffs**

List all setoffs made by any creditor, including a bank, against a debt or deposit of the debtor within 90 days preceding the commencement of this case. (Married debtors filing under chapter 12 or chapter 13 must include information concerning either or both spouses whether or not a joint petition is filed, unless the spouses are separated and a joint petition is not filed.)

Give NAME AND ADDRESS OR CREDITOR, DATE OF SETOFF and AMOUNT OF SETOFF.

☐ None   **14. Property Held for Another Person**

List all property owned by another person that the debtor holds or controls.

Give NAME AND ADDRESS OF OWNER, DESCRIPTION AND VALUE OF PROPERTY and LOCATION OF PROPERTY.

☐ None   **15. Prior Address of Debtor**

If the debtor has moved within the two years immediately preceding the commencement of this case, list all premises which the debtor occupied during that period and vacated prior to the commencement of this case. If a joint petition is filed, report also any separate address of either spouse.

Give ADDRESS, NAME USED and DATES OF OCCUPANCY.

☐ None   **16. Spouses and Former Spouses**

If the debtor resides or resided in a community property state, commonwealth, or territory (including Alaska, Arizona, California, Idaho, Louisiana, Nevada, New Mexico, Puerto Rico, Texas, Washington, or Wisconsin) within the six-year period immediately preceding the commencement of the case, identify the name of the debtor's spouse and of any former spouse who resides or resided with the debtor in the community property state.

Give NAME.

☐ None   **17. Environmental Information**

For the purpose of this question, the following definitions apply: "Environmental Law" means any federal, state, or local statute or regulation regulating pollution, contamination, releases of hazardous or toxic substances, wastes or material into the air, land, soil, surface water, groundwater, or other medium, including, but not limited to, statutes or regulations regulating the cleanup of these substances, wastes, or material. "Site" means any location, facility, or property as defined under any Environmental Law, whether or not presently or formerly owned or operated by the debtor, including, but not limited to, disposal sites. "Hazardous Material" means anything defined as a hazardous waste, hazardous substance, toxic substance, hazardous material, pollutant, or contaminant or similar term under an Environmental Law.

☐ None   **a.** List the name and address of every site for which the debtor has received notice in writing by a governmental unit that it may be liable or potentially liable under or in violation of an Environmental law. Indicate the governmental unit, the date of the notice, and, if know, the Environmental Law:

Give SITE NAME AND ADDRESS, NAME AND ADDRESS OF GOVERNMENTAL UNIT, DATE OF NOTICE and ENVIRONMENTAL LAW.

☐ None   **b.** List the name and address of every site for which the debtor has provided notice to a governmental unit of a release of Hazardous Material. Indicate the governmental unit to which the notice was sent and the date of the notice.

Give SITE NAME AND ADDRESS, NAME AND ADDRESS OF GOVERNMENTAL UNIT, DATE OF NOTICE and ENVIRONMENTAL LAW.

☐ None   **c.** List all judicial or administrative proceedings, including settlements or orders, under any Environmental Law with respect to which the debtor is or was a party. Indicate the name and address of the governmental unit that is or was a party to the proceeding, and the docket number.

Give NAME AND ADDRESS OF GOVERNMENTAL UNIT, DOCKET NUMBER and STATUS OR DISPOSITION.

18. Nature, Location and Name of Business

☐ None   **a.** If the debtor is an individual, list the names and addresses of all businesses in which the debtor was an officer, director, partner, or managing executive of a corporation, partnership, sole proprietorship or was a self-employed professional within the two years immediately preceding the commencement of this case, or in which the debtor owned 5 percent or more of the voting or equity securities within the two years immediately preceding the commencement of this case.

b. If the debtor is a partnership, list the names and addresses of all businesses in which the debtor was a partner or owned 5 percent or more of the voting securities, within the two years immediately preceding the commencement of this case.

c. If the debtor is a corporation, list the names and addresses of all businesses in which the debtor was a partner or owned 5 percent or more of the voting securities within the two years immediately preceding the commencement of this case.

Give NAME, ADDRESS, NATURE OF BUSINESS and BEGINNING AND ENDING DATES OF OPERATION.

The following questions are to be completed as shown below.*

19. Books, Records, and Financial Statements

☐ None   a. List all bookkeepers and accountants who within the six years immediately preceding the filing of this bankruptcy case kept or supervised the keeping of books of account and records of the debtor.

Give NAME AND ADDRESS and DATES SERVICE RENDERED.

☐ None   b. List all firms or individuals who within the two years immediately preceding the filing of this bankruptcy case have audited the books of account and records, or prepared a financial statement of the debtor.

Give NAME, ADDRESS and DATES SERVICES RENDERED.

☐ None   c. List all firms or individuals who at the time of the commencement of this case were in possession of the books of account and records of the debtor. If any of the books of account and records are not available, explain.

Give NAME AND ADDRESS and DATE ISSUED.

☐ None   d. List all financial institutions, creditors and other parties, including mercantile and trade agencies, to whom a financial statement was issued within the two years immediately preceding the commencement of this case by the debtor.

Give NAME AND ADDRESS and DATE ISSUED.

20. Inventories

☐ None   a. List the dates of the last two inventories taken of your property, the name of the person who supervised the taking of each inventory, and the dollar amount and basis of each inventory.

Give DATE OF INVENTORY, INVENTORY, SUPERVISOR and DOLLAR AMOUNT OF INVENTORY (specify cost, marketor other basis).

☐ None   b. List the name and address of the person having possession of the records of each of the two inventories reported in a., above.

Give DATE OF INVENTORY and NAME AND ADDRESSES OF CUSTODIAN OF INVENTORY RECORDS.

21. Current Partners, Officers, Directors and Shareholders

☐ None   a. If the debtor is a partnership, list the nature and percentage of partnership interest of each member of the partnership.

Give NAME AND ADDRESS, NATURE OR INTEREST and PERCENTAGE OF THE INTEREST.

☐ None   b. If the debtor is a corporation, list all officers and directors of the corporation, and each stockholder who directly or indirectly owns, controls, or holds 5 percent or more of the voting securities of the corporation.

Give NAME AND ADDRESS, TITLE and NATURE AND PERCENTAGE OF STOCK OWNERSHIP.

22. Former Partners, Officers, Directors and Shareholders

☐ None   a. If the debtor is a partnership, list each member who withdrew from the partnership within one year immediately preceding the commencement of this case.

Give NAME, ADDRESS and DATE OF WITHDRAWAL.

☐ None   b. If the debtor is a corporation, list all officers or directors whose relationship with the corporation terminated within one year immediately preceding the commencement of the case.

Give NAME AND ADDRESS, TITLE and DATE OF TERMINATION.

23. Withdrawals from a Partnership or Distributions by a Corporation

☐ None If the debtor is a partnership or corporation, list all withdrawals or distributions credited or given to an insider, including compensation in any form, bonuses, loans, stock redemption, options exercised and any other perquisite during one year immediately preceding the commencement of this case.

Give NAME & ADDRESS OF RECIPIENT, RELATIONSHIP TO DEBTOR, DATE AND PURPOSE OR WITHDRAWAL, and AMOUNT OF MONEY OR DESCRIPTION AND VALUE OR PROPERTY.

24. Tax Consolidation Group.

☐ If the debtor is a corporation, list the name and federal taxpayer identification number of the parent corporation of any consolidated group for tax purposes of which the debtor has been a member at any time within the six-year period immediately preceding the commencement of the case.

Give NAME OF PARENT CORPORATION and TAXPAYER IDENTIFICATION NUMBER.

25. Pension Funds.

☐ If the debtor is not an individual, list the name and federal taxpayer identification number of any fund to which the debtor, as an employer, has been responsible for contributing at any time within the six-year period immediately preceding the commencement of the case.

Give NAME OF PENSION FUND and TAXPAYER IDENTIFICATION NUMBER.

_____continuation sheets attached

Complete unsworn declaration on page 3076-5

* The following questions are to be completed by every debtor that is a corporation or partnership and by any individual debtor who is or has been, within the six years immediately preceding the commencement of this case, any of the following: an officer, director, managing executive, or owner of more than 5 percent of the voting securities or a corporation; a partner, other than a limited partner, of a partnership; a sole proprietor or otherwise self-employed. *(An individual or joint debtor should complete this portion of the statement only if the debtor is or has been in business, as defined above, within the six years immediately preceding the commencement of this case. A debtor who has not been in business within those six years should directly to the signature page.)*

[If completed by an individual or individual and spouse]

I declare under penalty of perjury that I have read the answers contained in the foregoing statement of financial affairs and any attachments thereto and that they are true and correct.

Date ———————————   Signature ————————————————————
                               of Debtor

Date ———————————   Signature ————————————————————
                               of Joint Debtor
                               (if any)

···

[If completed on behalf of a partnership or corporation]

I, declare under penalty of perjury that I have read the answers contained in the foregoing statement of financial affairs and any attachments thereto and that they are true and correct to the best of my knowledge, information and belief.

Date ———————————   Signature ————————————————————

                                       ————————————————————
                                       Print Name and Title

[An individual signing on behalf of a partnership or corporation must indicate position or relationship to debtor.]

————— continuation sheets attached.

Penalty for making a false statement: Fine of up to $500,000 or imprisonment for up to 5 years, or both. 18 U.S.C. §§152 and 3571.

···

CERTIFICATION AND SIGNATURE OF NON-ATTORNEY BANKRUPTCY PETITION PREPARER (See 11 U.S.C. § 110)

I certify that I am a bankruptcy petition preparer as defined in 11 U.S.C. § 110, that I prepared this document for compensation, and that I have provided the debtor with a copy of this document.

————————————————————————   ————————————————
Printed or Typed Name of Bankruptcy Petition Preparer   Social Security No.

————————————————————

————————————————————
Address

Names and Social Security numbers of all other individuals who prepared or assisted in preparing this document: If more than one person prepared this document, attach additional signed sheets conforming to the appropriate Official Form for each person.

X————————————————————   ————————————
Signature of Bankruptcy Petition Preparer   Date

A bankruptcy petition preparer's failure to comply with the provisions of title II and the Federal Rules of Bankruptcy Procedure may result in fines or imprisonment or both. 18 U.S.C. § 156.

Blumberg's Law Products Form B6 (6-90)

Julius Blumberg, Inc. NYC 10013

UNITED STATES BANKRUPTCY COURT   **DISTRICT OF**

In re: Debtor(s)   Case No.   (If Known)

See summary below for the list of schedules. Include Unsworn Declaration under Penalty of Perjury at the end.

GENERAL INSTRUCTIONS: Schedules D, E and F have been designed for the listing of each claim only once. Even when a claim is secured only in part, or entitled to priority only in part, it still should be listed only once. A claim which is secured in whole or in part should be listed on Schedule D only, and a claim which is entitled to priority in whole or in part should be listed in Schedule E only. Do not list the same claim twice. If a creditor has more than one claim, such as claims arising from separate transactions, each claim should be scheduled separately.

Review the specific instructions for each schedule before completing the schedule.

SUMMARY OF SCHEDULES

Indicate as to each schedule whether that schedule is attached and state the number of pages in each. Report the totals from Schedules A, B, D, E, F, I and J in the boxes provided. Add the amounts from Schedules A and B to determine the total amount of the debtor's assets. Add the amounts from Schedules D, E, and F to determine the total amount of the debtor's liabilities.

Name of Schedule	Attached (Yes No)	Number of sheets	Amounts Scheduled		
			Assets	Liabilities	Other
A - Real Property					
B - Personal Property					
C - Property Claimed as Exempt					
D - Creditors Holding Secured Claims					
E - Creditors Holding Unsecured Priority Claims					
F - Creditors Holding Unsecured Nonpriority Claims					
G - Executory Contracts and Unexpired Leases					
H - Codebtors					
I - Current Income of Individual Debtor(s)					
J - Current Expenditures of Individual Debtor(s)					
Total Number of Sheets of All Schedules					
Total Assets					
Total Liabilities					

Blumbergs Law Products   Form B6 A/B, P1(6-90)   Julius Blumberg, Inc. NYC 10013

In re: Debtor(s)   Case No.   (if known)

SCHEDULE A - REAL PROPERTY

DESCRIPTION AND LOCATION OF PROPERTY	NATURE OF DEBTOR'S INTEREST IN PROPERTY	H W J C	CURRENT MARKET VALUE OF DEBTOR'S INTEREST IN PROPERTY WITHOUT DEDUCTING ANY SECURED CLAIM OR EXEMPTION	AMOUNT OF SECURED CLAIM

Total -> $

(Report also on Summary of Schedules.)

SCHEDULE B - PERSONAL PROPERTY

TYPE OF PROPERTY	N O N E	DESCRIPTION AND LOCATION OF PROPERTY	H W J C	CURRENT MARKET VALUE OF DEBTOR'S INTEREST IN PROPERTY WITHOUT DEDUCTING ANY SECURED CLAIM OR EXEMPTION
1. Cash on hand				
2. Checking, savings or other financial accounts, certificates of deposit, or shares in banks, savings and loan, thrift, building and loan, and homestead associations, or credit unions, brokerage houses, or cooperatives.				
3. Security deposits with public utilities, telephone companies, landlords, and others.				
4. Household goods and furnishings including audio, video and computer equipment.				
5. Books; pictures and other art objects; antiques; stamp, coin, record, tape, compact disc, and other collections or collectibles.				
6. Wearing apparel.				
7. Furs and jewelry.				
8. Firearms and sports, photographic, and other hobby equipment.				
9. Interests in insurance policies. Name insurance company of each policy and itemize surrender or refund value of each.				

3072 © 1991 JULIUS BLUMBERG, INC., NYC 10013

Form B6B, P2 (6-90)   Julius Blumberg, Inc. NYC 10013   **SCHEDULE B**
PERSONAL PROPERTY

In re: Debtor(s)   Case No.   (if known)

TYPE OF PROPERTY	N O N E	DESCRIPTION AND LOCATION OF PROPERTY	H W J C	CURRENT MARKET VALUE OF DEBTOR'S INTEREST IN PROPERTY WITHOUT DEDUCTING ANY SECURED CLAIM OR EXEMPTION
10. Annuities. Itemize and name each issuer.				
11. Interests in IRA, ERISA, Keogh, or other pension or profit sharing plans. Itemize				
12. Stock and interests in incorporated and unincorporated businesses. Itemize.				
13. Interest in partnerships or joint ventures. Itemize.				
14. Government and corporate bonds and other negotiable and nonegotiable instruments.				
15. Accounts receivable.				
16. Alimony, maintenance, support, and property settlements to which the debtor is or may be entitled. Give particulars.				
17. Other liquidated debts owing debtor including tax refunds. Give particulars.				
18. Equitable or future interests, life estates, and rights or powers exercisable for the benefit of the debtor other than those listed in Schedule of Real Property.				
19. Contingent and noncontingent interests in estate of a decedent, death benefit plan, life insurance policy, or trust.				
20. Other contingent and unliquidated claims of every nature, including tax refunds, counterclaims of the debtor, and rights to setoff claims. Give estimated value of each.				
21. Patents, copyrights, and other intellectual property. Give particulars.				
22. Licenses, franchises, and other general intangibles. Give particulars.				
23. Automobiles, trucks, trailers, and other vehicles and accessories.				
24. Boats, motors, and accessories.				
25. Aircraft and accessories.				
26. Office equipment, furnishings, and supplies.				
27. Machinery, fixtures, equipment, and supplies used in business.				
28. Inventory.				
29. Animals.				
30. Crops - growing or harvested. Give particulars.				
31. Farming equipment and implements.				
32. Farm supplies, chemicals, and feed.				
33. Other personal property of any kind not already listed. Itemize.				

(Include amounts from any continuation sheets attached. Report total also on Summary of Schedules)   Total -> $

_____ continuation sheets attached

3072 © 1991 JULIUS BLUMBERG, INC., NYC 10013

Form B6 C (6,90)

Julius Blumberg, Inc. NYC 10013

In re: Debtor(s)   Case No.   (if known)

SCHEDULE C - PROPERTY CLAIMED AS EXEMPT

Debtor elects the exemptions to which debtor is entitled under (Check one box)

☐ 11 U.S.C. § 522(b)(1): Exemptions provided in 11 U.S.C. § 522(d). Note: These exemptions are available only in certain states.

☐ 11 U.S.C. § 522(b)(2): Exemptions available under applicable nonbankruptcy federal laws, state or local law.

DESCRIPTION OF PROPERTY	SPECIFY LAW PROVIDING EACH EXEMPTION	VALUE OF CLAIMED EXEMPTION	CURRENT MARKET VALUE OF PROPERTY WITHOUT DEDUCTING EXEMPTION

3072 © 1991 JULIUS BLUMBERG, INC., NYC 10013

Form B6 D (6-90)   Julius Blumberg, Inc. NYC 10013

In re: Debtor(s)   Case No.   (if known)

SCHEDULE D - CREDITORS HOLDING SECURED CLAIMS

☐ Check this box if debtor has no creditors holding secured claims to report on this Schedule D.

CREDITOR'S NAME AND MAILING ADDRESS INCLUDING ZIP CODE	CO D E B T	H W J C	DATE CLAIM WAS INCURRED, NATURE OF LIEN, AND DESCRIPTION AND MARKET VALUE OF PROPERTY SUBJECT TO LIEN	C U D *	AMOUNT OF CLAIM WITHOUT DEDUCTING VALUE OF COLLATERAL	UNSECURED PORTION IF ANY
A/C #						
			VALUE $			
A/C #						
			VALUE $			
A/C #						
			VALUE $			
A/C #						
			VALUE $			
A/C #						
			VALUE $			
A/C #						
			VALUE $			
A/C #						
			VALUE $			
A/C #						
			VALUE $			
A/C #						
			VALUE $			

_____ continuation sheets attached

Subtotal -> $ _____
(Total of this page)

Total -> $ _____
(use only on last page)

*If contingent, enter C; if unliquidated, enter U; if disputed, enter D.

(Report total also on Summary of Schedules)

3072 © 1991 JULIUS BLUMBERG, INC., NYC 10013

Form B6 E (4/98)   BlumbergExcelsior Inc. NYC 10013

In re: Debtor(s)   Case No.   (if known)

SCHEDULE E - CREDITORS HOLDING UNSECURED PRIORITY CLAIMS

☐ Check this box if debtor has no creditors holding unsecured priority claims to report on this Schedule E

TYPE OF PRIORITY CLAIMS (Check the appropriate box(es) below if claims in that category are listed on the attached sheets)

☐ **Extensions of credit in an involuntary case**   Claims arising in the ordinary course of the debtor's business or financial affairs after the commencement of the case but before the earlier of the appointment of a trustee or the order for relief. 11 U.S.C. § 507 (a) (2).

☐ **Wages, salaries, and commissions**   Wages, salaries, and commissions, including vacation, severance, and sick leave pay owing to employees, and commissions owing to qualifying independent sales representatives up to $4,300* per person, earned within 90 days immediately preceding the filing of the original petition, or the cessation of business, whichever occurred first, to the extent provided in 11 U.S.C. § 507 (a) (3).

☐ **Contributions to employee benefit plans**   Money owed to employee benefit plans for services rendered within 180 days immediately preceding the filing of the original petition, or the cessation of business, whichever occurred first, to the extent provided in 11 U.S.C. § 507 (a) (4).

☐ **Certain farmers and fishermen**   Claims of certain farmers and fishermen, up to $4,300* per farmer or fisherman, against the debtor, as provided in 11 U.S.C. § 507 (a) (5).

☐ **Deposits by individuals**   Claims of individuals up to $1,950* for deposits for the purchase, lease, or rental of property or services for personal, family, or household use, that were not delivered or provided. 11 U.S.C. § 507 (a) (6).

☐ **Alimony, Maintenance, or Support**   Claims of a spouse, former spouse, or child of the debtor for alimony, maintenance, or support, to the extent provided in 11 U.S.C. § 507 (a) (7).

☐ **Taxes and Certain Other Debts Owed to Governmental Units**   Taxes, customs duties, and penalties owing to federal, state, and local governmental units as set forth in 11 U.S.C. § 507 (a) (8).

☐ **Commitments to Maintain the Capital of an Insured Depository Institution**   Claims based on commitments to the FDIC, RTC, Director of the Office of Thrift Supervision, Comptroller of the Currency, or Board of Governors of the Federal Reserve System, or their predecessors or successors, to maintain the capital of an insured depository institution. 11 U.S.C. § 507 (a) (9).

*Amounts are subject to adjustment on April 1, 1998, and every three years thereafter with respect to cases commenced on or after the date of adjustment.

CREDITOR'S NAME AND MAILING ADDRESS INCLUDING ZIP CODE	CO DEBT	H W J C	DATE CLAIM WAS INCURRED AND CONSIDERATION FOR CLAIM	C U D *	TOTAL AMOUNT OF CLAIM	AMOUNT ENTITLED TO PRIORITY
A/C#						
A/C#						
A/C#						
A/C#						
A/C#						

_____ Continuation sheets attached.

Subtotal -> (Total of this page) $

Total -> (use only on last page of the completed Schedule E) $

* If contingent, enter C; if unliquidated., enter U; if disputed , enter D.   (Report total also on Summary of Schedules)

Blumbergs Law Products   Form B6 E Cont. (6-90)   Julius Blumberg, Inc. NYC 10013

In re: Debtor(s)   Case No.   (if known)

SCHEDULE E - CREDITORS HOLDING UNSECURED PRIORITY CLAIMS
(Continuation Sheet)

CREDITOR'S NAME AND MAILING ADDRESS INCLUDING ZIP CODE	CO DEBT	H W J C	DATE CLAIM WAS INCURRED AND CONSIDERATION FOR CLAIM	C U D *	TOTAL AMOUNT OF CLAIM	AMOUNT ENTITLED TO PRIORITY
A/C #						
A/C #						
A/C #						
A/C #						
A/C #						
A/C #						
A/C #						
A/C #						
A/C #						

Sheet no. _____ attached to Schedule of Creditors Holding Priority Claims.

Subtotal -> $
(Total of this page)

Total -> $
(use only on last page of completed Schedule E.)

*If contingent, enter C; if unliquidated, enter U; if disputed, enter D.

(Report total also on Summary of Schedules)

3072 © 1991 JULIUS BLUMBERG. INC., NYC 10013

Form B6 F, 9-97   BlumbergExcelsior, Inc NYC 10013

In re: _____   Debtor(s)   Case No. _____   (if known)

SCHEDULE F - CREDITORS HOLDING UNSECURED NONPRIORITY CLAIMS

☐ Check this box if debtor has no creditors holding unsecured nonpriority claims to report on this Schedule F

CREDITOR'S NAME AND MAILING ADDRESS INCLUDING ZIP CODE	CODEBTOR	H W J C*	DATE CLAIM WAS INCURRED AND CONSIDERATION FOR CLAIM. IF CLAIM IS SUBJECT TO SETOFF, SO STATE.	C U D**	AMOUNT OF CLAIM
A/C #					
A/C #					
A/C #					
A/C #					
A/C #					
A/C #					
A/C #					
A/C #					
A/C #					

_____ Continuation Sheets attached.

Subtotal -> (Total of this page) $ _____

Total -> (use only on last page of completed Schedule F.) $ _____

* If husband, enter H; if wife, enter W; if joint enter J, if community, enter C.

** If contingent, enter C; if unliquidated, enter U; if disputed, enter D.

Form B6 F Cont., 9-97

Blumberg Excelsior, Inc NYC 10013

In re: _____ Debtor(s)   Case No. _____ (if known)

SCHEDULE F - CREDITORS HOLDING UNSECURED NONPRIORITY CLAIMS
(Continuation Sheet)

CREDITOR'S NAME AND MAILING ADDRESS INCLUDING ZIP CODE	CODEBTOR	H W J C.*	DATE CLAIM WAS INCURRED AND CONSIDERATION FOR CLAIM. IF CLAIM IS SUBJECT TO SETOFF, SO STATE.	C U D **	AMOUNT OF CLAIM
A/C #					
A/C #					
A/C #					
A/C #					
A/C #					
A/C #					
A/C #					
A/C #					
A/C #					

Sheet no. _____ of _____ sheets attached to Schedule of Creditors Holding Nonpriority Claims.

Subtotal -> $ _____
(Total of this page)

Total -> $ _____

* If husband, enter H; if wife, enter W; if joint enter J, if community, enter C.

** If contingent, enter C; if unliquidated, enter U; if disputed, enter D.

(use only on last page of completed Schedule F.)

3072 © 1997 JULIUS BLUMBERG, INC., NYC 10013

Form B6 G (6-90)   Julius Blumberg, Inc. NYC 10013

In re: Debtor(s)   Case No.   (if known)

SCHEDULE G - EXECUTORY CONTRACTS AND UNEXPIRED LEASES

☐ Check this box if debtor has no executory contracts or unexpired leases.

NAME AND MAILING ADDRESS, INCLUDING ZIP CODE, OF OTHER PARTIES TO LEASE OR CONTRACT.	DESCRIPTION OF CONTRACT OR LEASE AND NATURE OF DEBTOR'S INTEREST. STATE WHETHER LEASE IS FOR NONRESIDENTIAL REAL PROPERTY. STATE CONTRACT NUMBER OF ANY GOVERNMENT CONTRACT.

3072 © 1991 JULIUS BLUMBERG, INC., NYC 10013

Form B6 H, (6-90)   Julius Blumberg, Inc. NYC 10013

In re: Debtor(s)   Case No.   (if known)

SCHEDULE H - CODEBTORS

☐ Check this box if debtor has no codebtors.

NAME AND ADDRESS OF CODEBTOR	NAME AND ADDRESS OF CREDITOR

Form B6 Cont. (12/94)   Julius Blumberg, Inc. NYC 10013

In re: _____   Debtor(s)   Case No. _____

                                                              (if known)

DECLARATION CONCERNING DEBTOR'S SCHEDULES

DECLARATION UNDER PENALTY OF PERJURY BY INDIVIDUAL DEBTOR

I declare under penalty of perjury that I have read the foregoing summary and schedules, consisting of _____ sheets, and that they are true and correct to the best of my knowledge, information, and belief.

(Total shown on summary page plus 1.)

Date _____   Signature: _____
                                               Debtor

Date _____   Signature: _____
                            (Joint Debtor, if any) (If joint case, both spouses must sign.)

CERTIFICATION AND SIGNATURE OF NON-ATTORNEY BANKRUPTCY PETITION PREPARER (SEE 11 U.S.C. § 110)

I certify that I am a bankruptcy petition preparer as defined in 11 U.S.C. § 110, that I prepared this document for compensation, and that I have provided the debtor with a copy of this document.

_____   _____
Printed or Typed Name of Bankruptcy Petition Preparer   Social Security No.

_____
Address

Names and Social Security numbers of all other individuals who prepared or assisted in preparing this document:

If more than one person prepared this document, attach additional signed sheets conforming to the appropriate Official Form for each person.

X _____   _____
Signature of Bankruptcy Petition Preparer   Date

A bankruptcy petition preparer's failure to comply with the provisions of title 11 and the Federal Rules of Bankruptcy Procedure may result in fines or imprisonment or both. 11 U.S.C. § 110; 18 U.S.C. § 156

DECLARATION UNDER PENALTY OF PERJURY ON BEHALF OF A CORPORATION OR PARTNERSHIP

I, the _____ (the president or other officer or an authorized agent of the corporation or a member or an authorized agent of the partnership) of the _____ (corporation or partnership) named as debtor in this case, declare under penalty of perjury that I have read the foregoing summary and schedules, consisting of _____ sheets, and that they are true and correct to the best of my knowledge, information, and belief.   (Total shown on summary page plus 1.)

Date _____   Signature: _____
                            (Print or type name of individual signing on behalf of debtor.)

(An individual signing on behalf of a partnership or corporation must indicate position or relationship to debtor.)

3085   Statement of compensation: Rule 2016(b), 8-91   ⬤   Blumbergs Law Products   ⬤

UNITED STATES BANKRUPTCY COURT   **DISTRICT OF**

In re   Debtor(s)   Case No.   (If Known)

STATEMENT
Pursuant to Rule 2016(b)

The undersigned, pursuant to Rule 2016(b) Bankruptcy Rules, states that:

   (1) The undersigned is the attorney for the debtor(s) in this case.
   (2) The compensation paid or agreed to be paid by the debtor(s) to the undersigned is:
      (a) for legal services rendered or to be rendered in contemplation of and in connection
         with this case $ ....
      (b) prior to filing this statement, debtor(s) have paid $ ....
      (c) the unpaid balance due and payable is $ ....
   (3) $ of the filing fee in this case has been paid.
   (4) The services rendered or to be rendered include the following:
      (a) analysis of the financial situation, and rendering advice and assistance to the debtor(s) in determining whether to file a
         petition under title 11 of the United States Code.
      (b) preparation and filing of the petition, schedules, statement of affairs and other documents required by the court.
      (c) representation of the debtor(s) at the meeting of creditors.

   (5) The source of payments made by the debtor(s) to the undersigned was from earnings, wages and compensation for services
      performed, and

   (6) The source of payments to be made by the debtor(s) to the undersigned for the unpaid balance remaining, if any, will be from
      earnings, wages and compensation for services performed, and

   (7) The undersigned has received no transfer, assignment or pledge of property except the following for the value stated:

   (8) The undersigned has not shared or agreed to share with any other entity, other than with members of undersigned's law firm,
      any compensation paid or to be paid except as follows:

Dated: Respectfully submitted, ...*Attorney for Petitioner*

Attorney's name and address...

Initial Debtors Package for Chapter 11 Debtors

U.S. Department of Justice

Office of the United States Trustee

Southern and Western Districts of Texas
Region 7

Southern District Offices
Houston, Galveston, Laredo & Victoria Divisions
Bob Casey Federal Building, Suite 3516
515 Rusk Avenue   (713) 718-4650
Houston, Texas 77002   FAX (713) 718-4670

Corpus Christi, McAllen & Brownsville Divisions:
Wilson Plaza West, Suite 1107
606 N. Carancahua Street   (361) 888-3261
Corpus Christi, Texas 78476   FAX (361) 888-3263

DATE

FIELD(Attorney)
FIELD(Firm)
FIELD(AttAdrs1)
FIELD(AttAdrs2)
FIELD(AttCtyStZip)

Re: INITIAL REPORT TO THE UNITED STATES TRUSTEE FOR: **FIELD(DebtNm1)**,
CASE NUMBER: *FIELD(Case No.)*, AND INITIAL DEBTOR CONFERENCE DATE:
FIELD(IDC_Date) @ FIELD(IDC_Time)

TO THE DEBTOR AND DEBTOR'S ATTORNEY:

Debtor and counsel are to appear at a meeting in the Office of the U.S. Trustee on the above date and time. Pursuant to FRBP 2015, the U.S. Trustee requires that each Chapter 11 Debtor must complete and submit an "Initial Report" to the U.S. Trustee no later than five (5) days prior the above date set for the "Initial Debtor Conference". Failure to timely submit a complete report will result in necessity for you to appear at an additional conference to secure compliance and will require you to make an additional trip to our office. The United States Trustee may waive the Initial Debtor Conference in instances where the Initial Report as well as all additional information and schedules are complete and submitted to the United States Trustee at least five (5) days prior to the above date set for the Initial Debtor Conference. Your cooperation will ensure that this case gets off to a good start and improve the likelihood that the debtor will successfully emerge from Chapter 11 without unnecessary delays or expense.

Enclosed are the following items:

A.   Initial Report. The enclosed Chapter 11 Initial Report Checklist, the Initial Report Exhibit A and Exhibits B through G must be completed and submitted to the United States Trustee no later than five (5) days prior to the above date set for the Initial Debtor Conference. (Refer to Guidelines, Section V.) The following items are to be included in the "Initial Report":

   (1) Bank Account Declaration. Exhibit B. Proof of Closing of all pre-petition accounts should be attached. (i.e., a copy of the final statement with a zero balance or a letter from the bank). Proof that properly styled Debtor-in-Possession accounts have been opened should also be attached. (i.e., a copy of a voided check or bank signature card).

Page 2
Initial Report to U.S. Trustee
DATE

(2) <u>Insurance Statement</u>. Exhibit C. Please furnish a copy of the "Declaration Page" of the policy which should provide that the United States Trustee will be notified in the event of cancellation or non-renewal.

(3) <u>Projected 90-Day Profit and Loss Statement</u>. Exhibit D. Debtors must provide a three (3) month projection for operations following the date the petition was filed.

(4) <u>Certification of Receipt of Guidelines</u>. Exhibit E. <u>Designation and Acceptance of Responsible Individual</u>. Exhibits F and G. The debtor, or his representative in the case of a corporate debtor must certify that he has received a copy of the United States Trustee's Guidelines for Debtors' in Possession, agrees to comply with the guidelines and the person responsible for discharging the duties of a Debtor in Possession has accepted those responsibilities.

(5) <u>Federal Income Tax Returns</u> for the past three (3) years and for each year during the pendency of your case.

(6) <u>Sales tax returns</u> for the preceding three (3) months.

(7) <u>Financial Statements</u> issued by the debtor for the past three years and/or copies of financial statements given to lending institutions or private lenders within the past three years.

(8) If a debtor in possession is a corporation, a copy of a <u>corporate resolution</u> allowing the filing of the Chapter 11 petition and designating an individual to sign pleadings.

(9) If debtor in possession is a <u>partnership</u>, a copy of written agreement to the filing of this bankruptcy case by all partners, or by all general partners if debtor in possession is a limited partnership.

(10) <u>Real estate and personal property tax receipts</u> for the preceding three (3) years, if applicable.

B.   <u>Guidelines For Debtors-in-Possession</u>.
Debtors-in-Possession should carefully review these guidelines with their attorney so that they will understand what is expected by the U.S. Trustee.

C.   <u>Monthly Operating Reports with Instructions and Examples</u>. This report must be completed each month based on a calendar month, signed by the debtor, filed with the court, and served upon the United States Trustee by the 20th of the following month. (Refer to Section VII of Guidelines.)

Page 3
Initial Report to U.S. Trustee
DATE

PLEASE BE SURE TO HAVE THE PREPARER OF THESE REPORTS ATTEND THE INITIAL DEBTOR CONFERENCE IN ORDER TO INSURE COMPLIANCE WITH THE REPORTING REQUIREMENTS.

PLEASE NOTE:

PLEASE BE ADVISED THAT DISCLOSURE STATEMENTS, PLANS OF REORGANIZATION, ORDERS APPROVING SAME AND AMENDMENTS THEREOF MUST INCLUDE LANGUAGE REGARDING REPORTING REQUIREMENTS AS FOLLOWS:

> **The [reorganized debtor or other responsible party] shall be responsible for timely payments of fees incurred pursuant to 28 U.S.C. §1930(a)(6). After confirmation, the [reorganized debtor or other responsible party] shall file with the court and serve on the Unites States Trustee a monthly financial report for each month (or portion thereof) the case remains open in a format prescribed by the UST and provided to the debtor by the UST."**

D.   Designated Bank List. Immediately upon filing the Petition, all pre-petition bank accounts are required to be closed and new debtor-in-possession operating and tax accounts opened only at an Authorized Depository. A list of these institutions is enclosed. (Refer to Guidelines, Section III Information regarding bank accounts).

E.   Chapter 11 Quarterly Fee Payment(form). This is a form to use when making an amended or initial payment for Quarterly Fees to the United States Trustee. In subsequent quarters the debtor should receive an invoice from Atlanta, Georgia, for the minimum fee of $250.00 owed each quarter. If an invoice has not been received by the debtor after the initial calendar quarter then the debtor should contact our office immediately. (Refer to Guidelines, Section 8 Quarterly Fees). Quarterly fees are based on disbursements from the bankruptcy estate during a calendar quarter. Quarterly fees will accrue from the inception of the Chapter 11 case and continue to accrue beyond the confirmation of the plan of reorganization and until the United States Bankruptcy Court issues a FINAL DECREE or in the event that the case is DISMISSED or CONVERTED to anther chapter.

Pursuant to Bankruptcy Rule 1007(b), the debtor is required to file the following documents within fifteen (15) days of the petition date or request an extension from the court within that period:

PLEASE NOTE;

> **Schedules A through J**
> **Statement of Financial Affairs**
> **Mailing Matrix**

In addition, pursuant to Bankruptcy Rule 1007(d), <u>a list of the 20 largest unsecured creditors is required to be filed with the petition.</u> PLEASE SEE THAT THE CREDITORS ON THIS LIST ARE NOT RELATED PARTIES OR INSIDERS TO THE DEBTOR. Please ensure that the debtor is in compliance with Bankruptcy Rule 1007 and that you promptly serve a copy of all documents on the United States Trustee, **including the mailing matrix.**. (Refer to Guidelines, Page

Page 4
Initial Report to U.S. Trustee
DATE

Section IX, Notice requirements on the United States Trustee).

If you have any questions, please contact me at (361) 888-3261.

Yours truly,

UNITED STATES TRUSTEE

By: _____
                    Trial Attorney

cc: Debtor (w/enclosures)
Enclosures:
Chapter 11 Initial Debtor Information Instruction Page w/(Initial Report)
Guidelines for Debtors In Possession
Blank Monthly Operating Report Form
Instructions for Filing Chapter 11 Monthly Operating Reports with Example
List of Approved Banks
Chapter 11 Quarterly Fee Payment(form)
Guidelines for Attorney/Accountant Retainer Funds
McDade Waiver
Disclosure of Intent to Use Taxpayer Identification

Page 5
Initial Report to U.S. Trustee
DATE

UNITED STATES TRUSTEE - REGION 7
CHAPTER 11 INITIAL DEBTOR INFORMATION INSTRUCTION PAGE

Initial Report information has been designed to provide the United States Trustee with basic information about the debtor and ensure that the debtor successfully emerges from Chapter 11 without unnecessary delays or expense. This Instruction Page is for debtor's information in preparing the various documents which will comprise the Initial Report.

The items to be included in the Initial Report are as follows:

1.   **Initial Report Checklist**.

2.   **Initial Report Summary.** Exhibit A consists of three (3) pages identifying areas of concern. All debtors should complete this document and provide supporting information relevant to these areas of concern (if applicable).

3.   **Bank Account Declaration of Debtor.** All pre-petition bank accounts are required to be closed as of the date the Petition is filed and new accounts opened with the proper style "Debtor-in-Possession" and case number. All debtors must declare on Exhibit B under penalty of perjury the location of their pre-petition and post-petition bank accounts. Debtors should provide verification of account designation(s) and number(s) and a sample copy of a voided check on each account. Include tax identification numbers.

4.   **Insurance Statement.** All debtors are required to declare the current status of their insurance policy(s) on Exhibit C.

5.   **Projected 90-Day Profit and Loss Statement.** Debtors must provide a three month projection on an accrual basis for operations following the date of the Order of Relief (Exhibit D).

6.   **Certification of Receipt of Operating Guidelines and Reporting Requirements.** All debtors are required to attest to their receipt of the operating guidelines and reporting requirements (Exhibit E). Counsel for the debtor must also sign this certification.

7.   **Designation and Acceptance of Individual Responsible for Discharging Debtor's Duties.** (Exhibit F). Debtors must designate the individual who will be responsible for discharging the duties of the debtor-in-possession trustee in this bankruptcy proceeding. This person will be expected to attend the 341(a) meeting of creditors, disclosure hearing, confirmation hearing, and other significant hearings convened in this case.

Page 6
Initial Report to U.S. Trustee
DATE

8. <u>**Designation and Acceptance of Individual Responsible for Preparation of Financial Reports for Debtor-in-Possession.**</u> (Exhibit G). Debtors must designate the individual who will be responsible for preparing all financial reports required by the Court or United States Trustee. This person will be expected to attend the 341(a) meeting of creditors, disclosure hearing, confirmation hearing, and any other significant hearings, convened in this case regarding the debtor's financial condition.

Page 7
Initial Report to U.S. Trustee
DATE

INITIAL REPORT CHECKLIST

CHAPTER 11

CASE NAME: FIELD(DebtNm1)
                  FIELD(DebtNm2)
                  FIELD(DebtNm3)

CASE NUMBER: FIELD(Case No.)

Please check items as appropriate:

_____ **Exhibit A,**   **Initial Report Summary** is completed and attached., as applicable to "Businesses" and/or "Apartment Complexes".

_____ **Exhibit B,**   **Bank Account Declaration** is completed and attached.

_____ **Exhibit C,**   **Insurance Statement** is completed and attached.

_____ **Exhibit D,**   **Projected 90-Day Profit And Loss Statement** is completed and attached.

_____ **Exhibit E,**   **Certification Of Receipt Of Guidelines For Debtors In Possession** is completed and attached.

_____ **Exhibit F,**   **Designation And Acceptance Of Individual Responsible For Discharging Debtor In Possession Duties** is completed and attached.

_____ **Exhibit G,**   **Designation And Acceptance Of Individual Responsible For Preparation Of Financial Reports For Debtor In Possession** is completed and attached.

Page 8
Initial Report to U.S. Trustee
DATE

Exhibit A

INITIAL REPORT SUMMARY

CASE NAME: FIELD(DebtNm1)

CASE NUMBER: FIELD(Case No.)

1. TYPE OF BUSINESS: _____

2. TYPE OF DEBTOR:

    CORPORATION_____PARTNERSHIP_____SOLE PROPRIETORSHIP_____

    NUMBER OF EMPLOYEES:____ DATE COMMENCED/INCORPORATED:_____

3. CORPORATE OFFICERS, PARTNERS, OR SOLE PROPRIETOR:

NAME	TITLE PERCENT OWNERSHIP	COMPENSATION (PAST 12 MONTHS)

    _____

    _____

4. LIST ALL INSIDERS AS DEFINED IN SECTION 101(31)(A)-(F) OF THE UNITED
STATES BANKRUPTCY CODE AND ANY COMPENSATION FOR THE LAST SIX
MONTHS:

    _____

    _____

    _____

    _____

    _____

    _____

Page 9
Initial Report to U.S. Trustee
DATE

5. CHAPTER 11 PETITION DATE: _____

   REASONS FOR FILING: _____

   _____

6. PROPOSED PLAN OF REORGANIZATION: _____

   _____

7. DATE PROPOSED PLAN OF REORGANIZATION TO BE FILED: _____

8. FINANCIAL CONDITION ON DATE OF FILING:

   TOTAL ASSETS:_____TOTAL DEBTS:_____

     CASH: _____INVENTORY:_____

     ACCOUNTS/NOTES RECEIVABLE:_____UNCOLLECTIBLE:_____

     ACCOUNTS/NOTES RECEIVABLE FROM INSIDERS:_____

     FIXTURES & EQUIPMENT:_____

     VEHICLES (TOTAL NUMBER AND VALUE): _____

     REAL ESTATE: _____

     _____

     <u>LOCATION/DESCRIPTION</u>
     <u>VALUE DEBT</u>   <u>LIEN HOLDER</u>

     _____

     _____

     _____

9. OTHER SIGNIFICANT ASSETS: _____

Page 10
Initial Report to U.S. Trustee
DATE

10. TAXES OWED:

<u>TAXING AUTHORITY</u>   /<u>AMOUNT</u>

_____

_____

_____

11. WAGES OWED: _____NUMBER OF CLAIMS:_____

12. RENT OWED: _____MONTHS IN ARREARS: _____

13. SECURED DEBTS (DO NOT REPEAT OBLIGATIONS LISTED UNDER REAL ESTATE):

<u>SECURED PARTY</u>   <u>AMOUNT</u>   <u>COLLATERAL</u>

_____

_____

_____

_____

_____

_____

14. UNSECURED DEBTS (TOTAL): _____

Page 11
Initial Report to U.S. Trustee
DATE

Exhibit A

INITIAL REPORT SUMMARY (FOR APARTMENT COMPLEXES)

CASE NAME: FIELD(DebtNm1)
CASE NUMBER: FIELD(Case No.)

1. NAME OF COMPLEX: _____

2. ADDRESS OF COMPLEX: _____

    _____

3. NUMBER OF UNITS: _____ OCCUPANCY RATE: _____ RENT RANGE:_____

4. TYPE OF DEBTOR:
    CORPORATION_____PARTNERSHIP_____SOLE PROPRIETORSHIP_____

    NUMBER OF EMPLOYEES:_____ DATE COMMENCED/INCORPORATED:_____

5. CORPORATE OFFICERS, PARTNERS, OR SOLE PROPRIETOR:

NAME	TITLE	PERCENT OWNERSHIP	SALARY (PAST 12 MONTHS)

6. NAME OF MANAGEMENT COMPANY: _____

7. ADDRESS OF MANAGEMENT COMPANY: _____

    _____

8. MANAGEMENT FEE: _____

9. REPRESENTATIVE OF MANAGEMENT COMPANY: _____

10. IS MANAGEMENT COMPANY RELATED TO DEBTOR IN ANY MANNER? (IF "YES", EXPLAIN): _____

    _____

11. REASONS FOR FILING CHAPTER 11 PETITION: _____

    _____

Page 12
Initial Report to U.S. Trustee
DATE

12. PROPOSED PLAN OF REORGANIZATION:_____

_____

13. DATE PROPOSED PLAN OF REORGANIZATION TO BE FILED: _____

14. FINANCIAL CONDITION ON DATE OF FILING:

   TOTAL ASSETS:_____TOTAL DEBTS:_____

   CASH: _____INVENTORY:_____

   ACCOUNTS/NOTES RECEIVABLE: _____UNCOLLECTIBLE:_____

   ACCOUNTS/NOTES RECEIVABLE FROM INSIDERS:_____

   FIXTURES & EQUIPMENT:_____

   VEHICLES (TOTAL NUMBER AND VALUE): _____

   REAL ESTATE: _____

   LOCATION/DESCRIPTION   LIEN HOLDER   VALUE
            DEBT

   _____

   _____

   _____

15. OTHER SIGNIFICANT ASSETS: _____

16. TAXES OWED:

   TAXING AUTHORITY   AMOUNT

   _____

   _____

   _____

17. WAGES OWED: _____NUMBER OF CLAIMS:_____

18. RENT OWED: _____MONTHS IN ARREARS:_____

Page 13
Initial Report to U.S. Trustee
DATE

19. SECURED DEBTS: (DO NOT REPEAT OBLIGATIONS LISTED UNDER REAL
ESTATE):

<u>SECURED PARTY</u>   <u>AMOUNT</u>   <u>COLLATERAL</u>

_____

_____

_____

_____

_____

_____

20. UNSECURED DEBTS (TOTAL): _____

Page 14
Initial Report to U.S. Trustee
DATE

Exhibit B

BANK ACCOUNT DECLARATION

CASE NAME: FIELD(DebtNm1)

CASE NUMBER: FIELD(Case No.)

All pre-petition bank accounts of the debtor in possession in the above-referenced case, as listed below, were closed on (date) _____:

DEPOSITORY	ACCOUNT NAME	ACCOUNT NUMBER
_____	_____	_____
_____	_____	_____
_____	_____	_____

All cash which is property of the estate has been deposited in the following debtor in possession bank accounts:

DEPOSITORY	ACCOUNT NAME	ACCOUNT NUMBER
_____	_____	_____
_____	_____	_____
_____	_____	_____

DECLARATION UNDER PENALTY OF PERJURY

I declare under penalty of perjury that the information provided above and on any attachment hereto is true and correct to the best of my information and belief.

Date_____   Signature_____
                                    Debtor In Possession

                                    _____
                                    Print Name and Title

Page 15
Initial Report to U.S. Trustee
DATE

Exhibit C

INSURANCE STATEMENT

CASE NAME: FIELD(DebtNm1)

CASE NUMBER: FIELD(Case No.)

Insurer	Type	Coverage Amount	Policy Number	Expiration Date	Paid Through

DECLARATION UNDER PENALTY OF PERJURY

I declare under penalty of perjury that the information provided above and on any attachments hereto is true and correct to the best of my information and belief.

Date_____   Signature_____
                                                    Debtor In Possession

                                                    _____
                                                    Print Name and Title

Page 16
Initial Report to U.S. Trustee
DATE

Exhibit D

PROJECTED 90-DAY PROFIT AND LOSS STATEMENT
(Accrual Basis)

CASE NAME: **FIELD(DebtNm1)**
CASE NUMBER: **FIELD(Case No.)**   20____

	Month	Month	Month
Sales:			
Gross Sales			
Less: Returns/discounts	( )	( )	( )
Net Sales			
Cost of Goods Sold:			
Beginning Inventory at Cost			
Purchases			
Less: Ending Inventory at Cost			
Cost of Goods Sold (COGS)			
Gross Profit (Sales Less COGS)			
Other Operating Income			
Operating Expenses:			
Officer/Mgmt Payroll			
Payroll - Other Employees			
Payroll Taxes			
Depreciation and Amortization			
Rental - Real Property			
Leases - Personal Property			
Repairs and Maintenance			
Insurance			
Telephone and Utilities			
Travel and Entertainment			
Misc. Operating Expenses			
Total Operating Expenses	( )	( )	( )
Net Gain/(Loss) from operations			
Non-Operating Income:			
Interest Income			
Net Gain on Sale of Assets			
Total Non-Operating Income			
Non-Operating Expenses:			
Interest Expense			
Legal and Professional			
Total Non-Operating Expenses	( )	( )	( )
NET INCOME/(LOSS)			

Page 17
Initial Report to U.S. Trustee
DATE

Exhibit E

CERTIFICATION OF RECEIPT OF GUIDELINES
FOR DEBTORS IN POSSESSION

Case Name: **FIELD(DebtNm1)**

Case Number: **FIELD(Case No.)**

I hereby certify that I have received the United States Trustee's Guideline's For Debtor's In Possession, that I have read and understand the guidelines, and agree to comply with the guidelines and the requirements set forth therein.

Date _____   Signature_____
                                          Debtor In Possession

                            _____
                                        Print Name and Title

The undersigned attorney for the debtor in possession, has read and reviewed with the debtor in possession the United States Trustee's Guidelines For Debtor In Possession.

Date _____   Signature_____
                                          Attorney for Debtor

Page 18
Initial Report to U.S. Trustee
DATE

Exhibit F

DESIGNATION AND ACCEPTANCE OF INDIVIDUAL RESPONSIBLE FOR DISCHARGING THE DUTIES OF THE DEBTOR IN POSSESSION

CASE NAME: FIELD(DebtNm1)

CASE NUMBER: FIELD(Case No.)

I hereby designate _____, as provided under FRBP 9001(5), as the individual responsible for discharging the duties of the debtor-in-possession under 11 U.S.C. §1107, and as may be required by the court or the United States Trustee.

Date_____   Signature_____
                                                         Debtor In Possession

                                                 _____
                                                         Print Name And Title

                                         Address_____

                                                 _____

                                         Telephone _____

ACCEPTANCE

Date_____   _____
                                         Signature of Designated Individual

                                 _____
                                         Print Name and Title

                         Address _____

                                 _____

                 Telephone _____

Page 19
Initial Report to U.S. Trustee
DATE

Exhibit G

DESIGNATION AND ACCEPTANCE OF INDIVIDUAL RESPONSIBLE FOR PREPARATION OF FINANCIAL REPORTS FOR DEBTOR-IN-POSSESSION

CASE NAME: FIELD(DebtNm1)

CASE NUMBER: FIELD(Case No.)

I, hereby designate_____, as the individual responsible for the preparation of all financial reports as required by the court or the United States Trustee. Should this individual cease to be responsible for the preparation of financial reports, the debtor-in-possession will promptly designate another individual by serving upon the United States Trustee an amended Designation and Acceptance of Individual Responsible For Preparation of Financial Reports For Debtor In Possession.

Date_____   Signature_____
                                        Debtor In Possession

ACCEPTANCE

Date_____   _____
                             Signature of Designated Individual

                             _____
                             Print Name and Title

                    Address _____

                             _____

                    Telephone _____

UNITED STATES BANKRUPTCY COURT
SOUTHERN DISTRICT OF TEXAS
FIELD(Division) DIVISION

CASE NAME: FIELD(DebtNm1)
                FIELD(DebtNm2)
                FIELD(DebtNm3)

Petition Date :   FIELD(Petition Date)

CASE NUMBER: FIELD(Case No.)

THIS REPORT IS FOR THE MONTH/YEAR (example: MAY/1995) OF _____
All Individual Debtor-In-Possession Checking, Savings, Brokerage
Accounts :
BANK NAME: ACCOUNT NO.::

1.
2.
3.
(attach list if needed)

All Non-Debtor-In-Possession Accounts:

BANK NAME: ACCOUNT NO.::

1.
2.
3.
(attach list if needed)

A copy of a reconciled statement should be attached for each and all accounts.

Total Disbursements from MOR-7   +   Total Disbursements from MFR-2   =   Total Disbursements
     (When the debtor is a sole proprietorship)   (When the debtor is an Individual)

Are all post-petition liabilities, including taxes, being paid within terms?   Yes   No

Have any pre-petition liabilities been paid ?   Yes   No   If so, explain _____

Are all U. S. Trustee Quarterly Fee Payments current?   Yes   No

What is the status of your Plan of Reorganization?

The **original** of this document **must be filed** with the United States Bankruptcy Court and a copy **must be sent** to the United States Trustee

I certify under penalty of perjury that the following complete
Monthly Financial Report (MFR), consisting of MFR-1 through
MFR-3 plus attachments, is true and correct.

SIGNED _____
              (ORIGINAL SIGNATURE)

ATTORNEY NAME: FIELD(Attorney)
FIRM: FIELD(Firm)
ADDRESS: FIELD(AttAdrs1)
ADDRESS: FIELD(AttAdrs2)
CITY, STATE, ZIP: FIELD(AttCtyStZip)
TELEPHONE: FIELD(AttTele)

MFR-1

This FORM is for **INDIVIDUALS ONLY**

Petition Date: FIELD(Petition Date)

CASE NUMBER: FIELD(Case No.)

CASE NAME: FIELD(DebtNm1) FIELD(DebtNm2) FIELD(DebtNm3)

CASH RECEIPTS AND DISBURSEMENTS	SCHEDULE I & J	MONTH	MONTH	MONTH	MONTH	MONTH	MONTH	MONTH
1. CASH - BEGINNING OF MONTH								
RECEIPTS								
2. Wages, Salary, Commissions (net)								
3. Rents, Royalties, Dividends, Interest								
4. Social Security, Pension, etc.								
5. Other (attach list)								
TOTAL RECEIPTS								
Draw from (Contribution to) Operation of Business MOR-								
DISBURSEMENTS								
6. Rent or Home Mortgage Payment								
7. Utilities (electric/gas, water, telephone)								
8. Home Maintenance (repairs and upkeep)								
9. Food, Clothing, Laundry, and Dry Cleaning								
10. Medical and Dental								
11. Transportation (not including car payment)								
12. Recreations, Clubs, and Entertainment								
13. Insurance (not included in wages or home mortgage)								
14. Taxes (not included in wages or home mortgage)								
15. Auto Payment								
16. Credit Cards								
17. Other (attach list)								
SUB-TOTAL DISBURSEMENTS (for Individual)								
18. PROFESSIONAL FEES								
19. U.S. TRUSTEE FEES								
TOTAL DISBURSEMENTS								
20. NET CASH FLOW								
21. CASH - END OF MONTH								

Revised:6/14/96

MFR-2

This FORM is for **INDIVIDUALS ONLY**

CASE NAME: FIELD(DebtNm1)
                  FIELD(DebtNm2)
                  FIELD(DebtNm3)

CASE NUMBER: FIELD(Case No.)

POST-PETITION LIABILITIES	MONTH	MONTH	MONTH	MONTH	MONTH	MONTH
SECURED:						
(attach list)						
TOTAL SECURED						
UNSECURED:						
(attach list)						
TOTAL UNSECURED						
TAXES:						
(attach list)						
TOTAL TAXES						
TOTAL POST-PETITION LIABILITIES (for Individual)						

MFR-3

Revised:6/14/96

UNITED STATES BANKRUPTCY COURT
SOUTHERN DISTRICT OF TEXAS
FIELD(Division) DIVISION

CASE NAME: FIELD(DebtNm1)
    FIELD(DebtNm2)
    FIELD(DebtNm3)

Petition Date: FIELD(Petition Date)

CASE NUMBER: FIELD(Case No.)

MONTHLY OPERATING REPORT SUMMARY FOR MONTH _____ YEAR _____

	MONTH			
REVENUES (MOR-6)				
INCOME BEFORE INT, DEPREC./TAX (MOR-6)				
NET INCOME (LOSS) (MOR-6)				
PAYMENTS TO INSIDERS (MOR-9)				
PAYMENTS TO PROFESSIONALS (MOR-9)				
TOTAL DISBURSEMENTS (MOR-8)				

The original of this document must be filed with the United States Bankruptcy Court and a copy must be sent to the United States Trustee

CIRCLE ONE

Are all accounts receivable being collected within terms?   Yes   No
Are all post-petition liabilities, including taxes, being paid within terms?   Yes   No
Have any pre-petition liabilities been paid?   Yes   No   If so, describe _____

Are all funds received being deposited into DIP bank accounts?   Yes   No
Were any assets disposed of outside the normal course of business?   Yes   No
If so, describe _____
Are all U. S. Trustee Quarterly Fee Payments current?   Yes   No
What is the status of your Plan of Reorganization ? _____

I certify under penalty of perjury that the following complete
Monthly Operating Report (MOR), consisting of MOR-1 through
MOR-9 plus attachments, is true and correct.

SIGNED _____

TITLE _____

(ORIGINAL SIGNATURE)

REQUIRED INSURANCE MAINTAINED
AS OF SIGNATURE DATE

		EXP. DATE
CASUALTY	YES( ) NO( )	_ _ / _ _ / _ _
LIABILITY	YES( ) NO( )	_ _ / _ _ / _ _
VEHICLE	YES( ) NO( )	_ _ / _ _ / _ _
WORKER'S	YES( ) NO( )	_ _ / _ _ / _ _
OTHER	YES( ) NO( )	_ _ / _ _ / _ _

ATTORNEY NAME: FIELD(Attorney)
FIRM: FIELD(Firm)
ADDRESS: FIELD(AttAdrs1)
ADDRESS: FIELD(AttAdrs2)
CITY, STATE, ZIP: FIELD(AttCtyStZip)
TELEPHONE: FIELD(AttTele)

MOR-1

CASE NAME: FIELD(DebtNm1)
FIELD(DebtNm2)
FIELD(DebtNm3)

CASE NUMBER: FIELD(Case No.)

COMPARATIVE BALANCE SHEETS

ASSETS	FILING DATE* FIELD(Petition	MONTH	MONTH	MONTH	MONTH	MONTH	MONTH	MONTH	MONTH
CURRENT ASSETS									
Cash									
Accounts Receivable, Net									
Inventory: Lower of Cost or Market									
Prepaid Expenses									
Investments									
Other									
TOTAL CURRENT ASSETS									
PROPERTY, PLANT&EQUIP, @ COST									
Less Accumulated Depreciation									
NET BOOK VALUE OF PP & E									
OTHER ASSETS:									
1. Tax Deposits									
2. Investments in Subs									
3.									
4. (attach list)									
TOTAL ASSETS									

*Per <u>Schedules</u> and <u>Statement of Affairs</u>

Revised:6/14/96

MOR-2

CASE NAME: FIELD(DebtNm1)
              FIELD(DebtNm2)
              FIELD(DebtNm3)

CASE NUMBER: FIELD(Case No.)

COMPARATIVE BALANCE SHEETS

LIABILITIES & OWNER'S EQUITY	FILING DATE* FIELD(Petition Date)	MONTH	MONTH	MONTH	MONTH	MONTH	MONTH	MONTH
LIABILITIES:								
POST-PETITION LIABILITIES (MOR-4)								
PRE-PETITION LIABILITIES:								
Notes Payable-Secured								
Priority Debt								
Federal Income Tax								
FICA/Withholding								
Unsecured Debt								
Other								
TOTAL PRE-PETITION LIABILITIES								
TOTAL LIABILITIES								
OWNERS'S EQUITY (DEFICIT):								
PREFERRED STOCK								
COMMON STOCK								
ADDITIONAL PAID-IN CAPITAL								
RETAINED EARNINGS: Filing Date								
RETAINED EARNINGS: Post Filing Date								
TOTAL OWNER'S EQUITY (NET WORTH)								
TOTAL LIABILITIES & OWNER'S EQUITY								

*Per Schedules and _Statement of Affairs_

Revised:6/14/96

MOR-3

CASE NAME: FIELD(DebtNm1)
FIELD(DebtNm2)
FIELD(DebtNm3)

CASE NUMBER: FIELD(Case No.)

SCHEDULE OF POST-PETITION LIABILITIES

	MONTH	MONTH	MONTH	MONTH	MONTH	MONTH
TRADE ACCOUNTS PAYABLE						
TAX PAYABLE:						
Federal Payroll Taxes						
State Payroll & Sales						
Ad Valorem Taxes						
Other Taxes						
TOTAL TAXES PAYABLE						
SECURED DEBT POST-PETITION						
ACCRUED INTEREST PAYABLE						
*ACCRUED PROFESSIONAL FEES:						
OTHER ACCRUED LIABILITIES:						
1.						
2.						
3.						
TOTAL POST-PETITION LIABILITIES (MOR-3)						

* Payment Requires Court Approval.

Revised:6/14/96

MOR-4

CASE NUMBER: FIELD(Case No.)

CASE NAME: FIELD(DebtNm1)
              FIELD(DebtNm2)
              FIELD(DebtNm3)

AGING OF POST-PETITION LIABILITIES
MONTH _____

DAYS	TOTAL	TRADE ACCTS	FED TAXES	STATE TAXES	AD-VALOREM, OTHER TAXES	OTHER
0-30						
31-60						
61-90						
91 +						
TOTAL						

AGING OF ACCOUNTS RECEIVABLE

MONTH					
0-30 DAYS					
31-60 DAYS					
61-90 DAYS					
91 + DAYS					
TOTAL					

Revised:6/14/96

MOR-5

CASE NAME: FIELD(DebtNm1)
FIELD(DebtNm2)
FIELD(DebtNm3)

CASE NUMBER: FIELD(Case No.)

STATEMENT OF INCOME (LOSS)

MONTH						FILING TO DATE
REVENUES (MOR-1)						
TOTAL COST OF REVENUES						
GROSS PROFIT						
OPERATING EXPENSES:						
Selling & Marketing						
General & Administrative						
Insiders Compensation						
Professional Fees						
Other (attach list)						
TOTAL OPERATING EXPENSES						
INCOME BEFORE INT, DEPR/TAX (MOR-1)						
INTEREST EXPENSE						
DEPRECIATION						
OTHER (INCOME) EXPENSE*						
OTHER ITEMS**						
TOTAL INT, DEPR & OTHER ITEMS						
NET INCOME BEFORE TAXES						
FEDERAL INCOME TAXES						
NET INCOME (LOSS) (MOR-1)						

Accrual Accounting Required, Otherwise Footnote With Explanation
* *Footnote Mandatory*
** *Unusual and/or infrequent item(s) outside the ordinary course of business; requires footnote*

MOR-6

Revised:6/14/96

CASE NAME: FIELD(DebtNm1)
FIELD(DebtNm2)
FIELD(DebtNm3)

CASE NUMBER: FIELD(Case No.)

CASH RECEIPTS AND DISBURSEMENTS	MONTH	MONTH	MONTH	MONTH	MONTH	MONTH	FILING TO DATE
1. CASH - BEGINNING OF MONTH							
RECEIPTS:							
2. CASH SALES							
3. COLLECTION OF ACCOUNTS RECEIVABLE							
4. LOANS & ADVANCES (attach list)							
5. SALE OF ASSETS							
6. OTHER (attach list)							
TOTAL RECEIPTS							
(Withdrawal)Contribution by Individual Debtor MFR-2*							
DISBURSEMENTS:							
7. NET PAYROLL							
8. PAYROLL TAXES PAID							
9. SALES, USE & OTHER TAXES PAID							
10. SECURED / RENTAL / LEASES							
11. UTILITIES							
12. INSURANCE							
13. INVENTORY PURCHASES							
14. VEHICLE EXPENSES							
15. TRAVEL & ENTERTAINMENT							
16. REPAIRS, MAINTENANCE & SUPPLIES							
17. ADMINISTRATIVE & SELLING							
18. OTHER (attach list)							
TOTAL DISBURSEMENTS FROM OPERATIONS							
19. PROFESSIONAL FEES							
20. U.S. TRUSTEE FEES							
21. OTHER REORGANIZATION EXPENSES (attach list)							
TOTAL DISBURSEMENTS							
22. NET CASH FLOW							
23. CASH - END OF MONTH (mor-2)							

MOR-7

*Applies to Individual debtor's only.

Revised: 6/14/96

CASE NAME: FIELD(DebtNm1)
              FIELD(DebtNm2)
              FIELD(DebtNm3)

CASE NUMBER: FIELD(Case No.)

CASH ACCOUNT RECONCILIATION
MONTH OF

BANK NAME					
ACCOUNT NUMBER	#		#		
ACCOUNT TYPE	OPERATING	PAYROLL	TAX	OTHER FUNDS	TOTAL
BANK BALANCE					
DEPOSIT IN TRANSIT					
OUTSTANDING CHECKS					
ADJUSTED BANK BALANCE					
BEGINNING CASH - PER BOOKS					
RECEIPTS					
TRANSFERS BETWEEN ACCOUNTS					
(WITHDRAWAL)CONTRIBUTION- BY INDIVIDUAL DEBTOR MFR-2					
CHECKS/OTHER DISBURSEMENTS					
ENDING CASH - PER BOOKS					

Revised:6/14/96

MOR-8

CASE NAME: FIELD(DebtNm1)
FIELD(DebtNm2)
FIELD(DebtNm3)

CASE NUMBER: FIELD(Case No.)

PAYMENTS TO INSIDERS AND PROFESSIONALS

Of the total disbursements shown for the month, list the amount paid to insiders (as defined in Section 101(31)(A)–(F) of the U. S. Bankruptcy Code) and the professionals. Also, for insiders identify the type of compensation paid (e.g., salary, commission, bonus, etc.) (Attach additional pages as necessary.)

INSIDERS: NAME/POSITION/COMP TYPE	MONTH	MONTH	MONTH	MONTH	MONTH	MONTH
1.						
2.						
3.						
4.						
5.						
6.						
TOTAL INSIDERS (MOR-1)						

PROFESSIONALS NAME/ORDER DATE	MONTH	MONTH	MONTH	MONTH	MONTH	MONTH
1.						
2.						
3.						
4.						
5.						
6.						
TOTAL PROFESSIONALS (MOR-1)						

Revised 6/14/96

MOR-9

U.S. Department of Justice
Office of the U.S. Trustee   **CHAPTER 11 QUARTERLY FEE PAYMENT**

Case Name: FIELD(DebtNm1)

Mailing Address: FIELD(DebtAdrs1), FIELD(DebtAdrs2), FIELD(DebtCtyStZip)

FIELD(Division), Texas   Ch. 11 ten-digit Account Number: IF(FIELD(Division)=BROWNSVILLE)INSERT(411)ELSE ENDIF IF(SUBSTR(FIELD(Division);1;3)=COR)INSERT(412)ELSE ENDIF IF(FIELD(Division)=GALVESTON)INSERT(413)ELSE ENDIF IF(FIELD(Division)=HOUSTON)INSERT(414)ELSE ENDIF IF(FIELD(Division)=LAREDO)INSERT(415) ELSE ENDIF IF(FIELD(Division)=VICTORIA)INSERT(416) ELSE ENDIF IF(FIELD(Division)=MCALLEN)INSERT(417) ELSE ENDIF - SUBSTR(FIELD(Case No.);1;2) - SUBSTR(FIELD(Case No.);4;5)
Court Location: City & State

Amount Enclosed: $_____

Mail this form and your payment to:
U.S. Trustee Payment Center
P.O. Box 198246, Atlanta, GA
                                        30384

[ ] Completed at U.S. Trustee Office

by:_____

Date Mailed _____ Signature * _____
* I certify under penalty of perjury that to the best of my knowledge this report is
correct.

                                        UST 11A 2/97

Cut Here   Cut Here

U.S. Department of Justice
Office of the U.S. Trustee   **CHAPTER 11 QUARTERLY FEE PAYMENT**

Case Name: FIELD(DebtNm1)

Mailing Address: FIELD(DebtAdrs1), FIELD(DebtAdrs2), FIELD(DebtCtyStZip)

FIELD(Division), Texas   Ch. 11 ten-digit Account Number: IF(FIELD(Division)=BROWNSVILLE)INSERT(411)ELSE ENDIF IF(SUBSTR(FIELD(Division);1;3)=COR)INSERT(412)ELSE ENDIF IF(FIELD(Division)=GALVESTON)INSERT(413)ELSE ENDIF IF(FIELD(Division)=HOUSTON)INSERT(414)ELSE ENDIF IF(FIELD(Division)=LAREDO)INSERT(415) ELSE ENDIF IF(FIELD(Division)=VICTORIA)INSERT(416) ELSE ENDIF IF(FIELD(Division)=MCALLEN)INSERT(417) ELSE ENDIF - SUBSTR(FIELD(Case No.);1;2) - SUBSTR(FIELD(Case No.);4;5)
Court Location: City & State

Amount Enclosed: $_____

Mail this form and your payment to:
U.S. Trustee Payment Center
P.O. Box 198246, Atlanta, GA
                                        30384

[ ] Completed at U.S. Trustee Office

by:_____

Date Mailed _____ Signature * _____
* I certify under penalty of perjury that to the best of my knowledge this report is
correct.

                                        UST 11A 2/97

Cut Here   Cut Here

U.S. Department of Justice
Office of the U.S. Trustee   **CHAPTER 11 QUARTERLY FEE PAYMENT**

Case Name: FIELD(DebtNm1)

Mailing Address: FIELD(DebtAdrs1), FIELD(DebtAdrs2), FIELD(DebtCtyStZip)

FIELD(Division), Texas   Ch. 11 ten-digit Account Number: IF(FIELD(Division)=BROWNSVILLE)INSERT(411)ELSE ENDIF IF(SUBSTR(FIELD(Division);1;3)=COR)INSERT(412)ELSE ENDIF IF(FIELD(Division)=GALVESTON)INSERT(413)ELSE ENDIF IF(FIELD(Division)=HOUSTON)INSERT(414)ELSE ENDIF IF(FIELD(Division)=LAREDO)INSERT(415) ELSE ENDIF IF(FIELD(Division)=VICTORIA)INSERT(416) ELSE ENDIF IF(FIELD(Division)=MCALLEN)INSERT(417) ELSE ENDIF - SUBSTR(FIELD(Case No.);1;2) - SUBSTR(FIELD(Case No.);4;5)
Court Location: City & State

Amount Enclosed: $_____

Mail this form and your payment to:
U.S. Trustee Payment Center
P.O. Box 198246, Atlanta, GA
                                        30384

[ ] Completed at U.S. Trustee Office

by:_____

Date Mailed _____ Signature * _____
* I certify under penalty of perjury that to the best of my knowledge this report is
correct.

                                        UST 11A 2/97

UNITED STATES TRUSTEE
REGION 7

Guidelines for Chapter 11 and Chapter 12
Attorney/Accountant Retainer Funds
Southern District of Texas

Pursuant to Bankruptcy Local Rule 2016(g), effective January 1, 1993, In Chapter 11 and Chapter 12 cases, all attorneys and accountants shall deposit retainer funds, whether received from the debtor, an insider or any third party, for and on behalf of work performed for the debtor in a depository authorized by the United States Trustee to hold and collateralize bankruptcy estate funds. The depository need not be the same depository utilized by the debtor in possession in the case for which the retainer funds were received . A copy of the current list of Approved Depositories may be obtained from the United States Trustee's Office.

A.   The attorney and/or accountant shall deposit all retainer funds in a separate account for each Chapter 11 or Chapter 12 case. The debtor in possession is not a required signatory on the account. Each account must be styled as follows:

   (Attorney or accountant name or firm name),   Trust account for

   (Debtor's name)   , Chapter 11 (or 12) Debtor in Possession

   Case No. _____

B.   For each Chapter 11 or 12 case, the attorney or accountant shall identify the depository, account name and account number where the retainer funds are located and advise either the United States Trustee (for Chapter 11 cases) or the Chapter 12 Trustee (for Chapter 12 cases) in writing prior to the sec. 341(a) meeting of creditors.

C.   These Guidelines shall not regulate whether the retainer account shall be interest-bearing and are not intended to relieve the attorney or accountant from any other professional or ethical obligation regarding client funds. All retainer accounts must comport with such rules and requirements.

D.   The banks will be advised by the United States Trustee to report monthly to your office on all such accounts.

UNITED STATES TRUSTEE

DATE

INITIAL DEBTOR CONFERENCE CHECKLIST

CASE NAME: FIELD(DebtNm1)
              FIELD(DebtNm2)

CASE NUMBER: FIELD(Case No.)

DATE OF FILING: FIELD(Petition Date)
DATE OF I.D.C.: FIELD(IDC_Date)   FIELD(IDC_Time)
341- FIELD(341 Date)   120-Day FIELD(120-Day)

FIELD(Attorney)   FIELD(AttTele)

_____

_____

	In Compliance		
PRELIMINARY QUESTIONS	Yes	NO	Due Date
1. HAS THE DEBTOR FILED **SCHEDULES AND SOFA?**			
2. DID THE DEBTOR **SIGN** THE SCHEDULES AND SOFA?			
3. DID THE DEBTOR **REVIEW AND UNDERSTAND** THE SCHEDULES AND SOFA THAT HE /SHE SIGNED?			
4. HAS THE DEBTOR **LISTED ALL ASSETS**, ALL PROPERTIES, ALL EXEMPT AND NON-EXEMPT ASSETS THAT HE IS AWARE OF?			
5. HAS THE DEBTOR **TRANSFERRED ANY ASSETS** WITHIN 1 YEAR BEFORE FILING?			
6. HAS THE DEBTOR MADE ANY **PREFERENTIAL PAYMENTS** TO ANY CREDITORS WITHIN 90 DAYS OF FILING?			
7. DOES THE DEBTOR HAVE ANY **INSURANCE CLAIMS** TO BE FILED?			
8. DOES THE DEBTOR HAVE ANY **LAWSUITS** AGAINST ANYONE? ANY **CHOSES IN ACTION?**			
9. DOES ANYONE **OTHER THAN THE DEBTOR HOLD ANY PROPERTY BELONGING TO THE DEBTOR?**			
10. LIST ANY AMENDMENTS TO SCHEDULES AND SOFA: _____ _____			
11. HAS DEBTOR FILED LIST OF **20 LARGEST UNSECURED** CREDITORS?			
12. HAS DEBTOR FILED STATEMENT OF **EXECUTORY CONTRACTS?**			
13. HAS INDIVIDUAL DEBTOR FILED SCHEDULE OF **CURRENT INCOME AND EXPENDITURES** (SCHEDULES I AND J)?			
14. HAS INDIVIDUAL DEBTOR FILED **LIST OF EXEMPTIONS (SCHEDULE C)?**			
15. HAS CORPORATE DEBTOR FILED LIST OF **EQUITY SECURITY HOLDERS** ACCORDING TO FRBP 1007(a) 3?			
16. HAS COUNSEL FILED HIS/HER **APPLICATION TO EMPLOY ATTORNEY?**			
17. HAS COUNSEL FILED **RULE 2016(B) DISCLOSURE OF COMPENSATION PAID TO ATTORNEY?**			
18. HAS DEBTOR FILED **APPLICATION TO EMPLOY** PROFESSIONAL?			
19. DOES DEBTOR ANTICIPATE THE NEED TO HIRE ANY OTHER PROFESSIONAL? NAME OF PROFESSIONAL_____			
20. THE **§341 FIRST MEETING OF CREDITORS** IS SCHEDULED FOR_____ ASCERTAIN THAT THE DEBTOR IS AWARE OF THIS MEETING INCLUDING DATE, TIME AND WHAT TO EXPECT.			
21. REVIEW THE CREDITORS SELECTED FOR THE CREDITORS COMMITTEE, FOR RELATED PARTIES, INSIDERS, SECURED CREDITORS. LIST ANY PROPOSED CHANGES TO CREDITOR COMMITTEE: _____ _____			
Notes: _____ _____ _____			

	In Compliance		
	Yes	NO	Due Date
UST INFORMATION REQUIRED AT IDC			
BANK ACCOUNTS:			
22. HAS DEBTOR **CLOSED** ALL PREPETITION ACCOUNTS?			
23. HAS DEBTOR PROVIDED **PROOF OF CLOSURE**?			
24. HAS DEBTOR **OPENED NEW DIP ACCOUNTS** FOR:			
OPERATIONS			
TAX			
PAYROLL			
PERSONAL			
OTHER			
25. HAS DEBTOR PROVIDED **PROOF OF OPENING** SUCH ACCOUNTS?			
26. ARE, ALL DIP ACCOUNTS **PROPERLY STYLED**?			
27. ARE ALL DIP ACCOUNTS AT AN **AUTHORIZED DEPOSITORY**?			
28. HAS THE DEBTOR COMPLETED AND RETURNED **EXHIBIT "B"**?			
29. INQUIRE AS TO ANY CASH COLLATERAL MOTIONS, ORDERS. HAS SEPARATE **CASH COLLATERAL ACCOUNT** BEEN ESTABLISHED?			
30. THE UST MAY GRANT AN EXCEPTION FOR USE OF A NON-AUTHORIZED DEPOSITORY UNDER CERTAIN CIRCUMSTANCES. IF THIS IS THE CASE, INFORM THE DEBTOR IT IS HIS RESPONSIBILITY TO HAVE AN OFFICIAL OF THE UNAUTHORIZED BANK CONTACT THE UST DIRECTLY FOR INSTRUCTIONS. THE DEBTOR IS TO PROVIDE THE UST WITH MONTHLY BANK STATEMENTS FROM UNAUTHORIZED BANKS UNTIL OTHERWISE INSTRUCTED			
INSURANCE			
31. ASK THE DEBTOR IF ALL INSURABLE ASSETS ARE INSURED AND COMPARE INSURED ASSETS TO SCHEDULED ASSETS?			
32. HAS DEBTOR PROVIDED **PROOF OF INSURANCE** ON ASSETS TO THE ESTATE?			
33. HAS DEBTOR COMPLETED AND RETURNED **EXHIBIT "C"**?			
34. WHAT KIND OF INSURANCE DOES THE DEBTOR HAVE?			
GENERAL LIABILITY			
PROPERTY DAMAGE			
VEHICLE			
WORKERS COMP			
OTHER			
35. THE UST IS TO BE **NOTIFIED** BY THE INSURANCE COMPANY **OF ANY CHANGES**, CANCELLATION OR EXPIRATION OF INSURANCE. LIST ANY INSURANCE THE DEBTOR **DOES NOT HAVE** OR THAT THE UST HAS DETERMINED THE DEBTOR			
FEDERAL INCOME TAX			
36. HAS THE DEBTOR PROVIDED THE **LAST THREE YEARS TAX RETURNS**?			
37. HAS AN **EXTENSION** BEEN FILED FOR THE CURRENT TAX RETURN?			
38. WHEN THE TAX RETURN IS FILED, THE UST IS TO RECEIVE A COPY. A COPY OF THE TAX RETURN IS TO BE FURNISHED TO THE UST FOR EACH YEAR THE CASE IS PENDING.)			
39. DOES THE DEBTOR EXPECT A **TAX REFUND**?			

Page 3

	In Compliance		
	Yes	NO	Due Date

SALES TAXES

40. IS THE DEBTOR CURRENT ON PAYING SALES TAXES? HAS THE DEBTOR PROVIDED THE THREE MOST RECENT SALES TAX RETURNS.

LICENSES

41. ARE THERE ANY **LICENSES** WHICH THE DEBTOR WOULD BE REQUIRED TO MAINTAIN IN HIS BUSINESS? (SUCH AS LIQUOR, REAL ESTATE, ETC.)

FINANCIAL STATEMENTS

42. HAVE THE **LAST 3 YEARS' FINANCIAL STATEMENTS** BEEN PROVIDED?

EXHIBITS D,E,F AND G

43. DID THE DEBTOR COMPLETE AND RETURN EXHIBITS D,E,F AND G?

44. DID THE DEBTOR RECEIVE THE OPERATING GUIDELINES? DOES HE UNDERSTAND DISCHARGING DEBTOR'S DUTY AND RESPONSIBILITY TO PREPARE AND TIMELY FILE COMPLETE AND ACCURATE FINANCIAL REPORTS.

OTHER QUESTIONS

45. IF THE DEBTOR IS A CORPORATION, HAS THE **CURRENT YEAR'S FRANCHISE TAX** BEEN PAID TO THE STATE?

46. IS THE CORPORATION **IN GOOD STANDING** WITH THE STATE.

47. IF THE DEBTOR IS A CORPORATION, HAS A **CORPORATE RESOLUTION** BEEN EXECUTED?

48. DOES THE UST HAVE A COPY.

49. HAS THE DEBTOR **FILED BANKRUPTCY BEFORE**. IF SO, LIST DATE OF FILING, CASE NUMBER AND FINAL DISPOSITION OF THE CASE.

50. DOES THE DEBTOR UNDERSTAND HOW TO COMPLETE THE MONTHLY OPERATING REPORT AND DOES THE DEBTOR UNDERSTAND THE DUE DATE FOR SAME (20TH DAY OF THE MONTH)?

UST REPORTING REQUIREMENTS

CAUSES FOR MOTIONS TO BE FILED:

FAILURE TO FILE MONTHLY OPERATING REPORT DUE ON THE 20TH OF EVERY MONTH (GO OVER USE OF IN-HOUSE FINANCIAL)

FAILURE TO PAY QUARTERLY FEES, BASED ON DISBURSEMENTS OUT OF THE ESTATE. IF THE DEBTOR VOLUNTARILY DISMISSES, FEES MUST BE PAID OR THE UST WILL OBJECT TO THE DISMISSAL. IF THE DEBTOR VOLUNTARILY CONVERTS, HE MUST LIST FEES OWED AS OF DATE OF CONVERSION ON CHAPTER 7 SCHEDULES, OR THE UST WILL FILE PROOF OF CLAIM.

FAILURE TO PAY POST-PETITION LIABILITIES.

FAILURE TO PAY POST-PETITION TAXES (UST MONITORS SUCH PAYMENTS).

PAYMENT OF PROFESSIONALS **WITHOUT FEE APPLICATION** AND ORDER FROM THE COURT.

FAILURE TO FILE DISCLOSURE STATEMENT AND PLAN WITHIN THE 120 DAY EXCLUSIVITY PERIOD.

CODE DOES NOT ALLOW THE FOLLOWING

THE DEBTOR IS NOT ALLOWED TO PAY ANY **PRE-PETITION LIABILITIES** WITHOUT AUTHORIZATION FORM THE COURT.

THE DEBTOR IS NOT ALLOWED TO **SELL ASSETS OUT OF THE ORDINARY COURSE OF BUSINESS** WITHOUT AUTHORIZATION FROM THE COURT.

THE DEBTOR IS NOT ALLOWED TO **OBTAIN POST-PETITION CREDIT** WITHOUT AUTHORIZATION FROM THE COURT.

SERVICES PERFORMED BY OR PAYMENT TO PROFESSIONALS WITHOUT COURT AUTHORIZATION.

Notes:

CASE NAME: FIELD(DebtNm1)

CASE NUMBER: FIELD(Case No.)

Communications by Office of the United States Trustee
Regarding Administrative Matters

Part I: Purpose

The United States Trustee is responsible for supervising the administration of cases under chapters 7, 11, 12, and 13 of the United States Bankruptcy Code. 28 U.S.C.§ 586: [To fulfill this responsibility, the United States Trustee has issued Guidelines for Debtors-in-Possession. The Guidelines impose certain administrative and reporting responsibilities on chapter 11 debtors-in-possession.]* In addition, debtors-in-possession must comply with certain statutory requirements such as a requirement to pay quarterly fees to the United States Trustee. 28 U.S.C. § 1930(a)(6). The local Office of the United States Trustee is available to assist debtors-in-possession in fulfilling these requirements. In addition, it is frequently necessary for the Office of the United States Trustee to contact debtors-in-possession concerning missing documents, incomplete forms, and other administrative matters.

Part II: WAIVER election

_____ The Office of the United States Trustee **MAY** contact my client directly concerning the administrative requirements of the United States Trustee. These requirements include the proper completion of operating reports, the maintenance of appropriate insurance, banking arrangements, and the payment of quarterly fees.

_____ The Office of the United States Trustee **MAY NOT** communicate directly with my client concerning the administrative requirements of the United States Trustee.

DATED:

_____
FIELD(Attorney)
FIELD(Firm)
FIELD(AttAdrs1)
FIELD(AttAdrs2)
FIELD(AttCtyStZip)

CASE NAME: FIELD(DebtNm1)

CASE NUMBER: FIELD(Case No.)

Communications by Office of the United States Trustee
Regarding Administrative Matters

Part I: Purpose

The United States Trustee is responsible for supervising the administration of cases under chapters 7, 11, 12, and 13 of the United States Bankruptcy Code. 28 U.S.C.§ 586: [To fulfill this responsibility, the United States Trustee has issued Guidelines for Debtors-in-Possession. The Guidelines impose certain administrative and reporting responsibilities on chapter 11 debtors-in-possession.]* In addition, debtors-in-possession must comply with certain statutory requirements such as a requirement to pay quarterly fees to the United States Trustee. 28 U.S.C. § 1930(a)(6). The local Office of the United States Trustee is available to assist debtors-in-possession in fulfilling these requirements. In addition, it is frequently necessary for the Office of the United States Trustee to contact debtors-in-possession concerning missing documents, incomplete forms, and other administrative matters.

Part II: WAIVER election

_____ The Office of the United States Trustee **MAY** contact my client directly concerning the administrative requirements of the United States Trustee. These requirements include the proper completion of operating reports, the maintenance of appropriate insurance, banking arrangements, and the payment of quarterly fees.

_____ The Office of the United States Trustee **MAY NOT** communicate directly with my client concerning the administrative requirements of the United States Trustee.

DATED:

_____
FIELD(Attorney)
FIELD(Firm)
FIELD(AttAdrs1)
FIELD(AttAdrs2)
FIELD(AttCtyStZip)

NOTICE

DISCLOSURE OF INTENT TO USE TAXPAYER IDENTIFYING NUMBER FOR THE PURPOSE OF COLLECTING AND REPORTING DELINQUENT QUARTERLY FEES OWED TO THE UNITED STATES TRUSTEE PURSUANT TO 28 U.S.C. 1930(A)(6)

Please be advised that, pursuant to the Debt Collection Improvements Act of 1996, Public Law 104-134, Title III, § 31001(i)(3)(A), 110 Stat. 1321-365, codified at 31 U.S.C. § 3701, the United States Trustee intends to use the debtor's Taxpayer Identifying Number ("TIN") as reported by the debtor or debtor's counsel in connection with the chapter 11 bankruptcy proceedings for the purpose of collecting and reporting on any delinquent debt, including chapter 11 quarterly fees, that are owed to the United States Trustee.

The United States Trustee will provide the debtor's TIN to the Department of Treasury for its use in attempting to collect overdue debts. Treasury may take the following steps: (1) submit the debt to the Internal Revenue Service Offset Program so that the amount owed may be deducted from any payment made by the federal government to the debtor, including but not limited to tax refunds; (2) report the delinquency to credit reporting agencies, (3) send collection notices to the debtor, (4) engage private collection agencies to collect the debt, and (5) engage the United States Attorney's office to sue for collection. Collection costs will be added to the total amount of the debt.

Reorganization under the Bankruptcy Code— Chapter 11

Public Information Series of the Bankruptcy Judges Division December 1998

> While the information presented herein is accurate as of the date of publication, it should not be cited or relied upon as legal authority. This information should not be used as a substitute for reference to the United States Bankruptcy Code (title 11, United States Code) and the Bankruptcy Rules, both of which may be reviewed at local law libraries, or to any local rules of practice adopted and disseminated by each bankruptcy court. Finally, this fact sheet should not substitute for the advice of competent legal counsel. For additional copies of this publication, please contact the Bankruptcy Judges Division, Administrative Office of the United States Courts (202) 502-1900.

A case filed under chapter 11 of the United States Bankruptcy Code is frequently referred to as a "reorganization" bankruptcy.

How Chapter 11 Works

A bankruptcy case commences when a bankruptcy petition is filed with the bankruptcy court. Fed. R. Bankr. P. 1002. A petition may be a voluntary petition, which is filed by the debtor, or it may be an involuntary petition, which is filed by creditors that meet certain requirements. 11 U.S.C. §§ 301, 303. A voluntary petition should adhere to the format of Form 1 of the Official Forms prescribed by the Judicial Conference of the United States. The Official Forms may be purchased at legal stationery stores or download from the internet at www.uscourts.gov. The voluntary petition will include standard information concerning the debtor's name(s), social security number or tax identification number, residence, location of principal assets (if a business), the debtor's plan or intention to file a plan, and a request for relief under the appropriate chapter of the Bankruptcy Code. In addition, the voluntary petition will indicate whether the debtor qualifies as a small business as defined in 11 U.S.C. § 101(51C) and whether the debtor elects to be considered a small business under 11 U.S.C. § 1121(e).

Upon the filing of a voluntary petition for relief under chapter 11 or, in an involuntary case, the entry of an order for such relief, the debtor automatically assumes an additional identity as the "debtor in possession." 11 U.S.C. § 1101. The term refers to a debtor that keeps possession and control of its assets while undergoing a reorganization under chapter 11, without the appointment of a case trustee. A debtor will remain a debtor in possession until the debtor's plan of reorganization is confirmed, the debtor's case is dismissed or converted to chapter 7, or a chapter 11 trustee is appointed. The appointment or election of a trustee occurs only in a small number of cases. Generally, the debtor, as "debtor in possession," operates the business and performs many of the functions that a trustee performs in cases under other chapters. 11 U.S.C. § 1107(a).

A written disclosure statement and a plan of reorganization must be filed with the court. 11 U.S.C. § 1121. The disclosure statement is a document that must contain information concerning the assets, liabilities, and business affairs of the debtor sufficient to enable a creditor to make an informed judgment about the debtor's plan of reorganization. 11 U.S.C. § 1125. The information required is governed by judicial discretion and the circumstances of the case. The contents of the plan must include a classification of claims and must specify how each class of claims will be treated under the plan. 11 U.S.C. § 1123. Creditors whose claims are "impaired," *i.e.,* those whose contractual rights are to be modified or who will be paid less than the full value of their claims under the plan, vote on the plan by ballot. 11 U.S.C. § 1126. After the disclosure statement is approved and the ballots are collected and tallied, the bankruptcy court will conduct a confirmation hearing to determine whether to confirm the plan. 11 U.S.C. § 1128.

The Chapter 11 Debtor in Possession

While individuals are not precluded from using chapter 11, it is more typically used to reorganize a business, which may be a corporation, sole proprietorship, or partnership. A corporation exists separate and apart from its owners, the stockholders. The chapter 11 bankruptcy case of a corporation (corporation as debtor) does not put the personal assets of the stockholders at risk other than the value of their investment in the company's stock. A sole proprietorship (owner as debtor), on the other hand, does not have an identity separate and distinct from its owner(s); accordingly, a bankruptcy case involving a sole proprietorship includes both the business and personal assets of the owners-debtors. Like a corporation, a partnership exists separate and apart from its partners. In a partnership bankruptcy case (partnership as debtor), however, the partners' personal assets may, in some cases, be used to pay creditors in the bankruptcy case or the partners may, themselves, be forced to file for bankruptcy protection.

Section 1107 of the Code places the debtor in possession in the position of a fiduciary, with the rights and powers of a chapter 11 trustee, and requires the performance of all but the investigative functions and duties of a trustee. These duties are set forth in the Bankruptcy Code and Federal Rules of Bankruptcy Procedure. 11 U.S.C. §§ 1106, 1107; Fed. R. Bankr. P. 2015(a). Such powers and duties include accounting for property, examining and objecting to claims, and filing informational reports as required by the court and the United States trustee, such as monthly operating reports. The debtor in possession also has many of the other powers and duties of a trustee including the right, with the court's approval, to employ attorneys, accountants, appraisers, auctioneers, or other professional persons to assist the debtor during its bankruptcy case. Other responsibilities include filing tax returns and filing such reports as are necessary or as the court orders after confirmation, such as a final accounting. The United States trustee is responsible for monitoring the compliance of the debtor in possession with the reporting requirements.

It should be noted that railroad reorganizations have specific requirements under subsection IV of chapter 11, which will not be addressed here, and that stock and commodity brokers are prohibited from filing under chapter 11 and are restricted to chapter 7. 11 U.S.C. § 109(d).

The Small Business Debtor

A small business is defined by the Bankruptcy Code as a person engaged in commercial or business activities (not including a person that primarily owns or operates real property) that has aggregate noncontingent, liquidated, secured, and unsecured debts that do not exceed $2,000,000. 11 U.S.C. § 101(51C). If a debtor qualifies and elects to be considered a small business under 11 U.S.C. § 1121(e), the case is put on a "fast track" and treated differently than a regular chapter 11 case under the Code. For example, the appointment of a creditors' committee and a separate hearing to approve the disclosure statement are not mandatory in a small business case. 11 U.S.C. § 1102(a)(3). The court may conditionally approve a disclosure statement, subject to final approval after notice and a hearing and solicitation of votes for acceptance or rejection of the plan. Thereafter, the disclosure statement hearing may be combined with the confirmation hearing. 11 U.S.C. § 1125(f). In addition, the debtor has a shortened period of time (100 days from the date of the order for relief) within which only the debtor may file a plan. After the 100-day period expires, any party in interest may file a plan; however, all plans must be filed within 160 days from the date of the order for relief. 11 U.S.C. § 1121(e).

The Single Asset Real Estate Debtor

Another type of debtor for which these are special provisions under the Bankruptcy Code is a single asset real estate debtor. The term "single asset real estate" is defined as "a single property or project, other than residential real property with fewer than four residential units, which generates substantially all of the gross income of a debtor and on which no substantial business is being conducted by a debtor" other than operating the real property and which has aggregate noncontingent liquidated secured debts of no more than $4,000,000. 11 U.S.C. § 101(51B). The Bankruptcy Code provides circumstances under which creditors of a single asset real estate debtor may obtain relief from the automatic stay which is not available to creditors in ordinary bankruptcy cases. 11 U.S.C. § 362(d). On request of a creditor with a claim secured by the single asset real estate and after notice and a hearing, the court will grant relief from the automatic stay to the creditor unless the debtor files a feasible plan of reorganization or begins making interest payments to the creditor within 90 days from the date of the order for relief. The interest payments must be equal to the current fair market interest rate on the value of the creditor's interest in the real estate. 11 U.S.C. § 362(d)(3).

The Automatic Stay

The automatic stay provides a period of time in which all judgments, collection activities, foreclosures, and repossessions of property are suspended and may not be pursued by the creditors on any debt or claim that arose before the filing of the bankruptcy petition. As with cases under other chapters of the Bankruptcy Code, a stay of creditor actions against the chapter 11 debtor automatically goes into effect when the bankruptcy petition is filed. 11 U.S.C. § 362(a). The filing of a petition, however, does not operate as a stay for certain types of actions listed under 11 U.S.C. § 362(b). The stay provides a breathing spell for the debtor, during which negotiations can take place to try to resolve the difficulties in the debtor's financial situation.

Under specific circumstances, the secured creditor can obtain an order from the court granting relief from the automatic stay. For example, when the debtor has no equity in the property and that property is not necessary for an effective reorganization, the secured creditor can seek an order of the court lifting the stay to permit the creditor to foreclose on the property, sell it, and apply the proceeds to the debt. 11 U.S.C. § 362(d).

It should be noted that, although creditors are stayed from action against the debtor unless relief is granted by the court, section 331 of the Bankruptcy Code permits applications for fees to be made by certain professionals during the case. Thus, a trustee, a debtor's attorney, or any professional person appointed by the court may apply to the court at intervals of 120 days for interim compensation and reimbursement payments. In very large cases with extensive legal work the court may permit more frequent applications. Although professional fees may be paid pursuant to authorization by the court, the debtor cannot make payments to professional creditors on prepetition obligations, *i.e.,* obligations which arose before the filing of the bankruptcy petition. The ordinary expenses of the ongoing business, however, continue to be paid.

Creditors' Committees

Creditors' committees can play a major role in chapter 11 cases. The United States trustee, a federal employee to be distinguished from a private case trustee or panel trustee, appoints the committee, which ordinarily consists of unsecured creditors who hold the seven largest unsecured claims against the debtor. 11 U.S.C. § 1102. The committee may consult with the debtor in possession on the administration of the case, investigate the conduct of the debtor and the operation of the business, and participate in the formulation of a plan. 11 U.S.C. § 1103. A creditor's committee may, with the court's approval, hire an attorney or other professionals to assist in the performance of the committee's duties. A creditors' committee can be an important safeguard to the proper management of the business by the debtor in possession.

Who Can File a Plan

There is no specific statutory time limit set for the filing of a plan; however, the debtor (unless a "small business" debtor, as set out above) has a 120-day period during which it has an exclusive right to file a plan. 11 U.S.C. § 1121(b). The debtor's exclusive period in which to file a plan may be extended or reduced by the court. After the exclusive period has expired, a creditor or the case trustee may file a competing plan. The United States trustee may not file a plan. 11 U.S.C. § 307.

A chapter 11 case may continue for many years unless the court, the United States trustee, the committee, or another party in interest acts to ensure the case's timely resolution. The creditors' right to file a competing plan provides incentive for the debtor to file a plan within the exclusive period and acts as a check on excessive delay in the case.

Avoidable Transfers

The debtor in possession or the trustee, as the case may be, has what are called "avoiding" powers. Such powers may be used to undo a transfer of money or property made during a certain period of time prior to the filing of the bankruptcy petition. By avoiding a particular transfer of property, the debtor in possession can cancel the transaction and force the return or "disgorgement" of the payments or property, which then are available to pay all creditors.

Generally, the power to avoid transfers is effective against transfers made within 90 days prior to the filing of the petition. However, transfers to insiders (*i.e.,* relatives, general partners, and directors or officers of the debtor) made up to a year prior to filing can be avoided. 11 U.S.C. §§ 101(31), 101(54), 547, 548. In addition, under 11 U.S.C. § 544, the trustee is given the authority to avoid transfers under applicable state law, which often provides for longer time periods. Avoiding powers are used, for example, to prevent unfair prepetition payments to one creditor at the expense of all other creditors.

Cash Collateral, Adequate Protection, and Operating Capital

Although the preparation, confirmation, and implementation of a plan of reorganization is at the heart of a chapter 11 case, other issues may arise which must be addressed by the debtor in possession. The debtor in possession may use, sell, or lease property of the estate in the ordinary course of its business, without prior approval, unless the court orders otherwise. 11 U.S.C. § 363(c). If the intended sale or use is outside the ordinary course of its business, the debtor must obtain permission from the court. A debtor in possession may not use "cash collateral," *i.e.,* collections of accounts subject to security interests or proceeds from the sale of pledged inventory or equipment, without the consent of the secured party or authorization by the court, which must first examine whether the interest of the secured party is adequately protected. 11 U.S.C. § 363.

When "cash collateral" is used (spent), the secured creditors are entitled to receive additional protection under section 363 of the Bankruptcy Code. Section 363 defines "cash collateral" as cash, negotiable instruments, documents of title, securities, deposit accounts, or other cash equivalents, whenever acquired, in which the estate and an entity other than the estate have an interest. It includes the proceeds, products, offspring, rents, or profits of property and the fees, charges, accounts or payments for the use or occupancy of rooms and other public facilities in hotels, motels, or other lodging properties subject to a creditor's security interest. The debtor in possession must file a motion requesting an order from the court authorizing the use of the cash collateral. Pending consent of the secured creditor or court authorization for the debtor's in possession's must segregate and account for all cash collateral in its possession. 11 U.S.C. § 363(c)(4). A party with an interest in property being used by the debtor may request that the court prohibit or condition this use to the extent necessary to provide "adequate protection" to the creditor.

Adequate protection may be required to protect the value of the creditor's interest in the property being used by the debtor in possession. This is especially important when there is a decrease in value of the property. The debtor may make periodic or lump sum cash payments, or provide an additional or replacement lien that will result in the creditor's property interest being adequately protected. 11 U.S.C. § 361.

When a chapter 11 debtor needs operating capital, it may be able to obtain it from a lender by giving the lender a court-approved "superpriority" over other unsecured creditors or a lien on property of the estate. 11 U.S.C. § 364.

Appointment or Election of a Case Trustee

Although the appointment of a case trustee is a rarity in a chapter 11 case, a party in interest or the United States trustee can request the appointment of a case trustee or examiner at any time prior to confirmation in a chapter 11 case. The court, on motion by a party in interest or the United States trustee and after notice and hearing, shall order the appointment of a case trustee for cause, including fraud, dishonesty, incompetence, or gross mismanagement, or if such an appointment is in the interest of creditors, any equity security holders, and other interests of the estate. 11 U.S.C. § 1104(a). The trustee is appointed by the United States trustee, after consultation with parties in interest and subject to the court's approval. Fed. R. Bankr. P. 2007.1. Alternatively, a trustee in a case may be elected if a party in interest requests the election of a trustee within 30 days after the court orders the appointment of a trustee. In that instance, the United States trustee convenes a meeting of creditors for the purpose of electing a person to serve as trustee in the case. 11 U.S.C. § 1104(b).

The case trustee is responsible for management of the property of the estate, operation of the debtor's business, and, if appropriate, the filing of a plan of reorganization. Section 1106 of the Code requires the trustee to file a plan "as soon as practicable" or, alternatively, to file a report explaining why a plan will not be filed or to recommend that the case be converted to another chapter or dismissed. 11 U.S.C. § 1106(a)(5).

The court, after notice and hearing, may, at any time before confirmation, upon the request of a party in interest or the United States trustee, terminate the trustee's appointment and restore the debtor to possession and management of the property of the estate and of the operation of the debtor's business. 11 U.S.C. § 1105.

The Role of an Examiner

The appointment of an examiner in a chapter 11 case is rare. The role of an examiner is generally more limited than that of a trustee. The examiner is authorized to perform the investigatory functions of the trustee and is required to file a statement of any investigation conducted. If ordered to do so by the court, however, an examiner may carry out any other duties of a trustee that the court orders the debtor in possession not to perform. 11 U.S.C. § 1106. Each court has the authority to determine the duties of an examiner in each particular case. In some cases, the examiner may file a plan of reorganization, negotiate or help the parties negotiate, or review the debtor's schedules to determine whether some of the claims are improperly categorized. Sometimes, the examiner may be directed to determine if objections to any proofs of claim should be filed or whether causes of action have sufficient merit so that further legal action should be taken. An the examiner may not serve as a trustee. 11 U.S.C. § 321.

The United States Trustee or Bankruptcy Administrator

In addition to the case trustee or examiner and the creditors' committee, the United States trustee plays a major role in monitoring the progress of a chapter 11 case and supervising its administration. The United States trustee is responsible for monitoring the debtor in possession's operation of the business, and the submission of operating reports and fees. Additionally, the United States trustee monitors applications for compensation and reimbursement by professionals, plans and disclosure statements filed with the court, and creditors' committees. The United States trustee conducts a meeting of the creditors, often referred to as the "section 341 meeting," in a chapter 11 case. 11 U.S.C. § 341. The United States trustee and creditors may question the debtor under oath at the section 341 meeting concerning the debtor's acts, conduct, property, and the administration of the case.

The United States trustee also imposes certain requirements on the debtor in possession concerning matters such as reporting its monthly income and operating expenses, the establishment of new bank accounts, and the payment of current employee withholding and other taxes. By law, the debtor in possession must pay a quarterly fee to the United States trustee for each quarter of a year until the case is converted or dismissed. 28 U.S.C. § 1930(a)(6). The amount of the fee, which may range from $250 to $10,000, depends upon the amount of the debtor's disbursements during each quarter. Should a debtor in possession fail to comply with the reporting requirements of the United States trustee or orders of the bankruptcy court or fail to take the appropriate steps to bring the case to confirmation, the United States trustee may file a motion with the court to have the debtor's chapter 11 case converted to a case under another chapter of the Code or to have the case dismissed.

It should be noted that in North Carolina and Alabama, bankruptcy administrators perform similar functions that United States trustees perform in the remaining forty-eight states. The bankruptcy administrator program is administered by the Administrative Office of the United States Courts, while the United States trustee program is administered by the Department of Justice. For purposes of this fact sheet, references to United States trustees are also applicable to bankruptcy administrators.

Motions

Prior to confirmation of a plan, there are several activities that may take place in a chapter 11 case. The continued operation of the debtor's business may lead to the filing of a number of contested motions. The most common are those seeking relief from the automatic stay, the use of cash collateral, or to obtain credit. There may also be litigation over executory (*i.e.,* unfulfilled) contracts and unexpired leases and the assumption or rejection of those executory contracts and unexpired leases by the debtor in possession. 11 U.S.C. § 365. Delays in formulating, filing, and obtaining confirmation of a plan often prompt creditors to file motions for relief from stay or motions to convert the case to a chapter 7 or to dismiss the case altogether.

Adversary Proceedings

Frequently, the debtor in possession will institute a lawsuit, known as an adversary proceeding, to recover money or property for the estate. Adversary proceedings may take the form of lien avoidance actions, actions to avoid preferences, actions to avoid fraudulent transfers, or actions to avoid post petition transfers. Such proceedings are governed by Part VII of the Federal Rules of Bankruptcy Procedure. At times, a creditors' committee may be authorized by the bankruptcy court to pursue these actions against insiders of the debtor if the plan provides for the committee to do so or if the debtor has refused a demand to do so. Creditors may also initiate adversary proceedings by filing complaints to determine the validity or priority of a lien, to revoke an order confirming a plan, to determine the dischargeability of a debt, to obtain an injunction, or to subordinate a claim of another creditor.

Claims

A claim is a right to payment or a right to an equitable remedy for a failure of performance if the breach gives rise to a right to payment. 11 U.S.C. § 101(5). In some instances, a creditor must file a proof of claim form along with documentation evidencing the validity and amount of the claim. When proofs of claim are required to be filed, creditors must file the proofs of claim with the bankruptcy clerk in the district where the case is pending. The clerk is required to keep a list of claims filed in a case when it appears that there will be a distribution to unsecured creditors. Fed. R. Bankr. P. 5003(b). Most creditors whose claims are scheduled (*i.e.,* claims listed by the debtor on the debtor's schedules), but not listed as disputed, contingent, or unliquidated, need not file claims because the schedule of liabilities is deemed to constitute evidence of the validity and amount of those claims. 11 U.S.C. § 1111. Any creditor whose claim is not scheduled or is scheduled as disputed, contingent, or unliquidated, must file a proof of claim in order to be treated as a creditor for purposes of voting on the plan and distribution under it. Fed. R. Bankr. P. 3003(c)(2). If a scheduled creditor chooses to file a claim, a properly filed proof of claim supersedes any scheduling of that claim. Fed. R. Bankr. P. 3003(c)(4). It is the responsibility of the creditor to determine whether the claim is accurately listed. The debtor must provide notification to those creditors whose names are added and whose claims are listed as a result of an amendment to the schedules. The notification also should advise such creditors of their right to file proofs of claim and that their failure to do so may prevent them from voting upon the debtor's plan of reorganization or participating in any distribution under that plan. When a debtor amends the schedule of liabilities to add a creditor or change the status of any claims to disputed, contingent, or unliquidated claims, the debtor must provide notice of the amendment to any entity affected. Fed. R. Bankr. P. 1009(a).

Equity Security Holders

An equity security holder is a holder of an equity security of the debtor. Examples of an equity security are a share in a corporation, an interest of a limited partner in a limited partnership, or a right to purchase, sell, or subscribe to a share, security, or interest of a share in a corporation or an interest in a limited partnership. 11 U.S.C. §§ 101(16), (17). An equity security holder may vote on the plan of reorganization and may file a proof of interest, rather than a proof of claim. A proof of interest is deemed filed for any interest that appears in the debtor's schedules, unless it is scheduled as disputed, contingent, or unliquidated. 11 U.S.C. § 1111. An equity security holder whose interest is not scheduled or scheduled as disputed, contingent, or unliquidated must file a proof of interest in order to be treated as a creditor for purposes of voting on the plan and distribution under it. Fed. R. Bankr. P. 3003(c)(2). A properly filed proof of interest supersedes any scheduling of that interest. Fed. R. Bankr. P. 3003(c)(4). Generally, most of the provisions that apply to proofs of claim, as discussed above, are also applicable to proofs of interest.

Conversion or Dismissal

A debtor in a case under chapter 11 has a one-time absolute right to convert the chapter 11 case to a case under chapter 7 unless (1) the debtor is not a debtor in possession, (2) the case originally was commenced as an involuntary case under chapter 11, or (3) the case was converted to a case under chapter 11 other than at the debtor's request. 11 U.S.C. § 1112(a). A debtor in a chapter 11 case does not have an absolute right to have the case dismissed upon request.

Generally, upon the request of a party in interest in the case or the United States trustee, after notice and hearing and "for cause," the court may convert a chapter 11 case to a case under chapter 7 or dismiss the case, whichever is in the best interest of creditors and the estate. 11 U.S.C. § 1112(b).

The court may convert or dismiss a case "for cause" when there is a continuing loss to the estate, an inability to effectuate a plan, unreasonable delay that is prejudicial to creditors, denial or revocation of confirmation, or inability to consummate a confirmed plan.

There are important exceptions to the conversion process in a chapter 11 case. One exception is that, unless the debtor requests the conversion, section 1112(c) of the Code prohibits the court from converting a case involving a farmer or charitable institution to a liquidation case under chapter 7.

The Disclosure Statement

The filing of a written disclosure statement is preliminary to the voting on a plan of reorganization, and the disclosure statement must provide "adequate information" concerning the affairs of the debtor to enable the holder of a claim or interest to make an informed judgment about the plan. 11 U.S.C. § 1125. After the disclosure statement is filed, the court must hold a hearing to determine whether the disclosure statement should be approved. Acceptance or rejection of a plan cannot be solicited without prior court approval of the written disclosure statement. 11 U.S.C. § 1125(b). After the disclosure statement has been approved, the debtor or proponent of a plan can begin to solicit acceptances of the plan, and creditors may also solicit rejections of the plan. Fed. R. Bankr. P. 3017(d) requires that, upon approval of a disclosure statement, the following must be mailed to the United States trustee and all creditors and equity security holders: (1) the plan, or a court approved summary of the plan; (2) the disclosure statement approved by the court; (3) notice of the time within which acceptances and rejections of the plan may be filed; and (4) such other information as the court may direct, including any opinion of the court approving the disclosure statement or a court-approved summary of the opinion. Fed. R. Bankr. P. 3017(d). In addition, the debtor must mail to the creditors and equity security holders entitled to vote on the plan or plans (1) notice of the time fixed for filing objections; (2) notice of the date and time for the hearing on confirmation of the plan; and (3) a ballot for accepting or rejecting the plan and, if appropriate, a designation for the creditors to identify their preference among competing plans. *Id.* However, in a small business case, the court may conditionally approve a disclosure statement subject to final approval after notice and a combined disclosure statement/plan confirmation hearing. 11 U.S.C. § 1125(f).

Acceptance of the Plan of Reorganization

As noted earlier, during the first 120-day period after the filing of the voluntary bankruptcy petition, which filing also acts as the order of relief, only the debtor in possession may file a plan of reorganization. The debtor in possession has 180 days after the filing of the voluntary petition (or in a case commenced by an involuntary petition, after the order for relief) to obtain acceptances of the plan. 11 U.S.C. § 1121. For cause, the court may extend or reduce this exclusive period. 11 U.S.C. § 1121(d). The exclusive right of the debtor in possession to file a plan is lost and any party in interest, including the debtor, may file a plan if and only if (1) a trustee has been appointed in the case, (2) the debtor has not filed a plan within the 120-day exclusive period or any extension granted by the court, or (3) the debtor has not filed a plan which has been accepted by each class of claims or interests that is impaired under the plan within the 180-day period or any extensions granted by the court. 11 U.S.C. § 1121.

If the exclusive period expires before the debtor has filed and obtained acceptance of a plan, other parties in interest in a case, such as the creditors' committee or a creditor, may file a plan. Such a plan may compete with a plan filed by another party in interest or by the debtor. If a trustee is appointed, the trustee is responsible for filing a plan, a report of why the trustee will not file a plan, or a recommendation for the conversion or dismissal of the case. 11 U.S.C. § 1106(a)(5). A proponent of a plan is subject to the same requirements as the debtor with respect to disclosure and solicitation.

It should be noted that, in a chapter 11 case, a liquidating plan is permissible. Such a plan often allows the debtor in possession to liquidate the business under more economically advantageous circumstances than a chapter 7 liquidation. It also permits the creditors to take a more active role in fashioning the liquidation of the assets and the distribution of the proceeds than in a chapter 7 case.

Section 1123(a) of the Bankruptcy Code lists the mandatory provisions of a chapter 11 plan and section 1123(b) lists the discretionary provisions. Section 1123(a)(1) provides that a chapter 11 plan shall designate classes of claims and interests for treatment under the reorganization. Generally, a plan will classify claim holders as secured creditors, unsecured creditors entitled to priority, general unsecured creditors, and equity security holders.

Under section 1126(c) of the Code, an entire class of claims accepts a plan if the plan is accepted by creditors that hold at least two-thirds in amount and more than one-half in number of the allowed claims in the class. Under section 1129(a)(10), if there are impaired classes of claims, the court cannot confirm a plan unless it has been accepted by at least one class of non-insiders who hold impaired claims (*i.e.,* claims that are not going to be paid completely or in which some legal, equitable, or contractual right is altered). Moreover, under section 1126(f), holders of unimpaired claims are deemed to have accepted the plan.

Under section 1127(a) of the Bankruptcy Code, the proponent may modify the plan at any time before confirmation, but the plan as modified must meet all the requirements of chapter 11. Federal Rule of Bankruptcy Procedure 3019 provides that, when there is a proposed modification after balloting has been conducted and the court finds after a hearing that the proposed modification does not adversely affect the treatment of any creditor who has not accepted the modification in writing, the modification shall be deemed to have been accepted by all creditors who previously accepted the plan. If it is determined that the proposed modification does have an adverse effect on the claims of nonconsenting creditors, then another balloting must take place.

Because more than one plan may be submitted to the creditors for approval, Federal Rule of Bankruptcy Procedure 3016(b) requires that every proposed plan and modification be dated and identified with the name of the entity or entities submitting such plan or modification. When competing plans are presented and meet the requirements for confirmation, the court must consider the preferences of the creditors and equity security holders in determining which plan to confirm.

Any party in interest may file an objection to confirmation of a plan. The Bankruptcy Code requires the court, after notice, to hold a hearing on the confirmation of a plan. If no objection to confirmation has been timely filed, the Code allows the court to determine that the plan has been proposed in good faith and according to law. Fed. R. Bankr. P. 3020(b)(2). Before confirmation can be granted, the court must be satisfied that there has been compliance with all the other requirements of confirmation set forth in section 1129 of the Code, even in the absence of any objections. In order to confirm the plan, the court must find that (1) the plan is feasible, (2) it is proposed in good faith, and (3) the plan and the proponent of the plan are in compliance with the Code. In addition, the court must find that confirmation of the plan is not likely to be followed by liquidation or the need for further financial reorganization.

The Discharge

While some courts have a practice of issuing a discharge order in a case involving an individual, a separate order of discharge is usually not entered in a chapter 11 case. Section 1141(d)(1) specifies that the confirmation of a plan discharges the debtor from any debt that arose before the date of confirmation. After the plan is confirmed, the debtor is required to make plan payments and is bound by the provisions of the plan of reorganization. The confirmed plan creates new contractual rights, replacing or superseding pre-bankruptcy contracts.

There are, of course, exceptions to the general rule that an order confirming a plan operates as a discharge. Confirmation of a plan of reorganization will discharge any type of debtor—corporation, partnership, or individual—from most types of prepetition debts. It does not, however, discharge an individual debtor from any debt made nondischargeable by section 523 of the Bankruptcy Code. Confirmation does not discharge the debtor if the plan is a liquidation plan, as opposed to one of reorganization, and the debtor is not an individual. When the debtor is an individual, confirmation of a liquidation plan will effect a discharge unless grounds would exist for denying the debtor a discharge if the case were proceeding under chapter 7 instead of chapter 11. 11 U.S.C. §§ 1141(d)(2), 727(a).

Postconfirmation Modification of the Plan

At any time after confirmation and before "substantial consummation" of a plan, the proponent of a plan may modify a plan if the modified plan would meet certain Bankruptcy Code requirements. 11 U.S.C. § 1127(b). This should be distinguished from preconfirmation modification of the plan. A modified postconfirmation plan does not automatically become the plan. A modified postconfirmation plan in a chapter 11 case becomes the plan only "if circumstances warrant such modification" and the court, after notice and hearing, confirms the plan as modified pursuant to chapter 11 of the Code.

Postconfirmation Administration

Federal Rule of Bankruptcy Procedure 3020(d) provides that, "[n]otwithstanding the entry of the order of confirmation, the court may issue any other order necessary to administer the estate." This authority would include the postconfirmation determination of objections to claims or adversary proceedings which must be resolved before a plan can be fully consummated. Sections 1106(a)(7) and 1107(a) of the Bankruptcy Code require a debtor in possession or a trustee to report on the progress made in implementing a plan after confirmation. A chapter 11 trustee or debtor in possession has a number of responsibilities to perform after confirmation, including consummating the plan, reporting on the status of consummation, and applying for a final decree.

Revocation of the Confirmation Order

A revocation of the confirmation order is an undoing or cancellation of the confirmation of a plan. A request for revocation of confirmation, if made at all, must be made by a party in interest within 180 days of confirmation. The court, after notice and hearing, may revoke a confirmation order "if and only if [the confirmation] order was procured by fraud." 11 U.S.C. § 1144.

The Final Decree

A final decree closing the case must be entered after the estate has been "fully administered." Fed. R. Bankr. P. 3022. Local bankruptcy court policies may determine when the final decree should be entered and the case closed.

Glossary

automatic stay A court injunction that bars creditors from pursuing any collection actions against your business after its bankruptcy has begun. The automatic stay ends when your business has completed its bankruptcy, its bankruptcy case is closed, a creditor gets permission to lift the stay in order to collect a debt, or your business's bankruptcy is dismissed.

bankruptcy A legal process for dealing with debt.

bankruptcy code The federal law that governs bankruptcy.

bankruptcy estate The assets owned by your business, including assets that it has an interest in.

bankruptcy petition The paperwork your business must file with the court to begin its bankruptcy.

bar date The date by which your business's creditors must file a proof of claim with the bankruptcy court after your business files for bankruptcy.

Chapter 7 liquidation bankruptcy In a Chapter 7, your business stops operating and its assets are sold in order to pay as much of what it owes as possible.

Chapter 11 reorganization bankruptcy A Chapter 11 bankruptcy gives your business an opportunity to restructure its debts under the protection of the bankruptcy court so that it can continue operating.

Chapter 13 bankruptcy A type of reorganization bankruptcy filed by individuals, including the owners of sole proprietorships.

claim A creditor's formal assertion in a bankruptcy that it is owed money by your business.

collateral When your business allows a creditor to put a lien on an asset that your business owns in exchange for extending credit to your business, that asset is collateral and the creditor with the lien is a secured creditor. The asset or collateral secures or guarantees your business's debt. In other words, if your business does not meet the terms of its agreement with the secured creditor, the creditor can take back the asset. The loss of a key asset can spell the end of your business.

confirmation   When the bankruptcy court approves your business's plan of reorganization in a Chapter 11 bankruptcy. Confirmation of the plan usually signals the end of the bankruptcy and the discharge or dismissal of any debts that your business will not pay according to the plan.

corporation   A form of business that is legally recognized as separate from its owners for the purposes of taxation, lawsuits, and contracts. A closely held corporation is not publicly traded and is owned by just a few people, even just one individual.

cramdown   The confirmation of a reorganization plan against the wishes of a business's creditors or class of creditors.

creditor   A business, individual, or government entity to whom your business owes money.

creditors meeting   This meeting, also called a *341 meeting,* occurs after your business's bankruptcy begins. At the meeting, you must answer questions, under oath, from the bankruptcy trustee and any of your business's creditors that decide to attend the meeting.

debt   A legal obligation to pay money to a business, individual, or government entity.

debtor in possession   A business in a Chapter 11 bankruptcy.

discharge   The bankruptcy court's cancellation of a debt in a personal bankruptcy.

disclosure statement   A written document prepared in a Chapter 11 bankruptcy that provides your business's creditors with enough information to evaluate its reorganization plan, so they can decide whether to vote for its approval.

equity   The market value of an asset, less any money that your business owes on it.

executory contract   A contract in which all parties to it have uncompleted obligations according to the contract. Once

one or both parties have fulfilled their contractual obligations, the contract is no longer executory.

exemption   The law that prohibits a creditor from taking an asset in order to satisfy a debt. Exemptions apply in personal, not business bankruptcies.

filing fee   The amount of money your business must pay to the court to begin its bankruptcy case.

foreclosure   A legal action by which a creditor takes a debtor's collateral in order to satisfy a debt.

general partnership   A type of business with two or more owners in which each owner has unlimited personal liability for the debts of the partnership.

general, unsecured claim   A creditor with this kind of claim does not have a lien on the debtor's asset. Therefore, the debt is not collateralized. Creditors with unsecured claims are less apt to get paid in a bankruptcy than creditors with secured claims.

judgment   A legal decision by the court in a lawsuit.

lien   The claim or legal right of a secured creditor to take an asset that your business owns, if your business does not pay the debt that is secured by the asset. For example, if a bank loaned your business money to purchase expensive machinery, the bank has a lien on that equipment and can take the machinery if your business does not repay the loan according to the terms of the loan agreement.

liquidation   The sale of your business's assets by the bankruptcy trustee in order to pay its debts in a Chapter 7 bankruptcy.

market value   The current value of an asset, or what it is worth today.

motion   A formal written request asking the court to do something. Two common motions in bankruptcy are a *motion to lift the automatic stay* and a *motion to dismiss.*

motion to lift the automatic stay   A motion filed by a secured creditor asking the court for permission to take back its collateral.

nonpurchase money security agreement A loan agreement signed by your business that gives one of its creditors a lien on an asset that your business owns.

priority debt A kind of debt that your business cannot discharge or erase through bankruptcy. Your business must pay the debt once its bankruptcy is over. Priority debts include past-due payroll taxes, other past-due taxes, and past-due wages owed to your business's employees.

proof of claims A document filed by a creditor in order to establish the creditor's right to be paid in a bankruptcy.

property An asset owned by your business, including real property (land and buildings), personal property (property that you own, not your business), tangible property (property you can see and touch), and intangible property (property that has value but that you cannot see or touch; goodwill, for example).

reaffirmation agreement An agreement in a personal Chapter 7 bankruptcy in which you promise to continue paying on a nondischargeable debt after your bankruptcy is over in order to keep the asset that secures the debt.

redemption agreement An agreement in a personal Chapter 7 bankruptcy in which you agree to pay the present value of an asset that you want to keep, not the amount that you owe on the debt related to the asset.

reorganization plan In a Chapter 11 bankruptcy, a reorganization plan details how your business intends to deal with its debts, among other things. Before your business can get out of bankruptcy, its reorganization plan must be approved by a majority of its creditors.

schedules Lists of your business's debts and assets that your business's attorney must file with the court along with your business's bankruptcy petition.

secured creditor A creditor with a lien on an asset.

security A synonym for collateral.

security interest A synonym for a lien.

sole proprietorship A legal form of business that makes no distinction between the business and its owner. Therefore, the owner of a sole proprietorship is legally responsible for all of the business's debts. In essence, the business is simply an extension of its owner.

statement of financial affairs A series of questions that your business must answer and file with the court.

trustee A federal government employee who monitors your business in a Chapter 11 bankruptcy, or a private individual who is appointed by the bankruptcy court to take control of your business's assets in a Chapter 7 bankruptcy.

unsecured creditor A creditor that does not have a lien on one of your business's assets.

wage garnishment A court order requiring an employer to pay a percentage of an employee's wages to the employee's creditor in order to satisfy a debt. Some states do not allow wage garnishment.

Resources

Bankruptcy

Bankruptcy Basics. Published by the Administrative Office of the United States Court, Bankruptcy Judges Division, this free, downloadable brochure explains the ins and outs of various types of bankruptcy, including Chapters 11 and 7. To download the brochure, go to <www.uscourts.gov/bankbasic.pdf>.

The Web site of the American Bankruptcy Institute, <www.abiworld.org>, is targeted toward bankruptcy attorneys and other bankruptcy experts. However, you can use the site to locate business bankruptcy attorneys in your area who have been certified by the American Board of Certification, the only national organization that certifies bankruptcy attorneys by specialty—business or consumer bankruptcy. You can also call the American Bankruptcy Institute at 703-739-1023 for attorney referrals.

Turnarounds

The Insiders Secrets to Saving Your Business: The Step-by-Step Turnaround Guide. This publication provides tools and techniques for planning and managing each phase of your business's turnaround, when you are convinced that you want to handle that process yourself. It is published by Turnaround Central and costs $197. It can be ordered on line at <www.turnaroundcentral.com/> or by calling 512-258-3104.

The Turnaround Management Association. This organization certifies turnaround professionals. To locate a certified turnaround professional in your area who can meet your particular needs, call the Association at 312-578-6900 or go to its Web site at <www.turnaround.org>.

Low-Cost/No-Cost Resources to Avoid a Bankruptcy or Turnaround

The Service Corps of Executives (SCORE). SCORE is a national nonprofit organization that is a resource partner with the federal Small Business Administration. SCORE is dedicated to the formulation, growth, and success of small businesses. Go to its Web site at <www.score.org> to receive online business counseling and advice, to locate the SCORE office nearest you, and to access how-to articles and other business resources. You can also call 800-634-0245 to get the address and phone number of a SCORE office in your area.

The Small Business Administration (SBA). The federal Small Business Administration helps entrepreneurs establish and run successful businesses. Go to its Web site at <www.sba.gov/> for contact information for the SBA office closest to you, to access an online library chock full of information related to laws and regulations that may apply to your business, for information about government programs your business may be able to benefit from, to learn about government and nongovernment small business resources and helpful publications, and much more.

Dealing with Stress and Coping with Your Emotions

Books

Mind Like Water: Keeping Your Balance in a Chaotic World, by Jim Ballard, John Wiley & Sons, 2002. This book provides easy-to-use strategies and techniques for staying calm and focused, no matter how many demands you are trying to juggle, how much stress you are under, and how much change is occurring in your life.

The Relaxation Response, by Herbert Benson, M.D., and Miriam Z. Klipper, Avon, 1990. This groundbreaking book on the mind-body connection was first published in 1975 and has since become a classic. Among other things, it explains the physical and mental benefits of meditation and teaches readers how to benefit from meditation.

CDs

The Waves of Relaxation: Guided Meditations and Stress Reduction Techniques to Promote Physical and Emotional Well-Being, by John Martin, MS MFT, and Suzanne Ciani. *The Gift of Relaxation, Stress Relief, Wellness,* by Barry Pitkoff, MS. These are two good relaxation CDs. Listen to them when you are in the car driving to or from work, or use them to help you fall asleep.

Videos

Yoga Zone: Conditioning and Stress and *Living Yoga's Stress Relief for Yoga for Beginners* are two good videos for those of you who know little or nothing about using yoga to relieve stress and to relax. The *Yoga Zone* video provides basic, easy-to-follow instructions for breathing, stretching, and simple yoga poses. The *Living Yoga* video, filmed on a beach in Maui, is just 20 minutes long, so it is a great way to relax your mind and muscles during your lunch hour or before or after a long day at the office. Both videos are available at Amazon.com and bookstores, as well as at stores that sell yoga supplies.

Web Sites

<www.jokes.com> or <www.ahajokes.com>. They say laughter is the best medicine, so when you are feeling down about your business, yuk it up at one of these Web sites. You will find thousands of jokes, plus cartoons and funny audios, as well as videos.

www.yoga.com. This Web site claims to be the world's largest resource for yoga, meditation, and wellness. Visit it to learn about various types of yoga, so that you can identify the best one for you and locate a yoga studio or teacher in your area. You can also purchase clothing to relax in, yoga and mediation CDs, videos, DVDs, books, and more at this site.

Index